Entrepreneur®
MAGAZINE'S

start*up*

Start Your Own

INFORMATION CONSULTANT BUSINESS

Your Step-by-Step Guide to Success

George Walsh and Alan Breznick
and Rachel Adelson

E**P**
Entrepreneur.
Press

Editorial Director: Jere L. Calmes
Managing Editor: Marla Markman
Cover Design: Beth Hansen-Winter
Production: Eliot House Productions
Composition: Ed Stevens

© 2004 by Entrepreneur Media Inc.

All rights reserved.

Reproduction or translation of any part of this work beyond that permitted by Section 107 or 108 of the 1976 United States Copyright Act without permission of the copyright owner is unlawful. Requests for permission or further information should be addressed to the Business Products Division, Entrepreneur Media Inc.

This publication is designed to provide accurate and authoritative information in regard to the subject matter covered. It is sold with the understanding that the publisher is not engaged in rendering legal, accounting, or other professional services. If legal advice or other expert assistance is required, the services of a competent professional person should be sought.

Library of Congress Cataloging-in-Publication Data

Walsh, George.
    Entrepreneur magazine's start your own information consultant business/by George Walsh, Alan Breznick, and Rachel Adelson.
    p.   cm.
    Includes index.
    ISBN 1-932156-73-9
    1. Information consultants. 2. Information services industry. 3. New business enterprises. I. Title: Start your own information consultant business. II. Breznick, Alan. III. Adelson, Rachel. IV. Entrepreneur (Irvine, Calif.) V. Entrepreneur magazine's how to become an information consultant. VI. Title.
    HD9999.I492E58 2004
    001'.068'1—dc22   2004046940

Printed in Canada

09 08 07 06 05 04   10 9 8 7 6 5 4 3 2 1

Contents

Preface vii

Chapter 1
Becoming a Know-It-All 1
    The Right Stuff 2
    The Thrill of the Search 2
    Finding Your Area of Expertise 5
    Who's in the Market for Information? 7
    What's That Information Worth? 9
    What Do You Need to Get Started? 9
    The Tools at Your Disposal 9

Chapter 2
Background Check: The Information Market 11
    Who Needs Information, and Why? 12
        Corporations Assessing Competition 12
        Corporations Preparing for
          Buyouts or Mergers 13
        Companies That Need Product Information 13
        Companies That Need Medical Information 13
        Individuals Researching Medical Conditions 13
        Individuals Looking for Personal Information . . . 14

Finding a Market for Your Services 14
Identifying the Competition 16
    The Information Explosion 17
    The Kindly (and Free) Librarian 17
    Inhouse Research Staffs 18
    Playing the Field 18

Chapter 3
FAQs **19**
    A Day in the Life 20
        9:00 A.M. Check Your E-Mail and Phone Messages 20
        9:30 A.M. Primary Research 21
        11:00 A.M. Contracts, Bills,
           Invoices, and Project Scheduling 22
        12:00 P.M. Lunch? 23
        12:30 P.M. Start Searching! 24
        2:30 P.M. Errands 24
        3:30 P.M. Search Some More 24
        5:00 P.M. Organize 24
        5:30 P.M. Miller Time! 24
    Structuring Your Business 25
        Teaming Up 26
        Subcontracting 26
        Big, Bigger, Biggest 27
        Hiring Employees 27
    Location, Location, Location 28
        The Homebased Business 28
        Exceptions to the Rule 29
        Face to Face 30
        Breaking the Law? 30
        Your Workspace 31
    Naming Your Business 32

Chapter 4
Gadgets and Gizmos **33**
    The Computer: Tool of Your Trade 34
    The Hard Drive: Choosing the Right-Size Toolbox 35
    RAM: Speed on the Fly 35
    The Eyes Have It 35
    CD-ROM Drives: Is Faster Better? 36
    Should You Get a Laptop? 36

Talking to the Digital World 37
Backup Devices and Firewalls: Better Safe than Sorry 38
Printers: Getting It on Paper 41
Facts by Fax 42
Do You Copy? 43
Scanners, Anyone? 43
Staying in Touch: Phone Lines 43
Paging Dr. Info... 44
Protecting Your Investments:
    Extended Warranties and Insurance 45

Chapter 5

Searching for Software **47**
The Basics: Web Access, E-Mail, and Word Processing 48
    Choosing an ISP 48
    Web Browsers 50
    E-Mail Programs 50
    Word Processors 51
Keeping House: Spreadsheets,
    Databases, and Contact Managers 52
    Spreadsheets: Just the Facts 52
    Database Software: Quick and Easy Data 53
    Contact Managers: People Data 53
Final Analysis: What You Need, and What It Costs 54
Other Software: Your Hard Drive Is the Limit 54

Chapter 6

Dollars and Sense **57**
Good Money after Bad 58
How Much Will You Spend? 58
Ouch! That Hurts! 59
Ongoing Costs 61
The Big Question: How Much Does It Pay? 62
    Charging Ahead: Figuring Your Hourly Worth 63
    Making the Bid: Flat Rate or Hourly? 65
    Billing 66
    Expected Annual Income 67

Chapter 7

What Do You Want to Know Today? **69**
Focusing Your Search 70

The Cheat Sheet 72
Start Your Engine 73
The Mathematics of Words 74
Just the Facts 77
Less Obvious Online Resources 78
Online Databases 79
Being Your Own Best Resource 79
Presentation Methods 80

Chapter 8
Good Exposure: Promoting Your Business 81

It's in the Cards 82
Snail Mail Potential 83
Does It Pay to Advertise? 86
The World Wide Web: Your Own Private Infomercial 87
Seizing the Limelight 88
See and Be Seen 89
Serving Up the Information 90
On Your Desk Every Tuesday Morning 90
Selling Your Smarts on the Web 92

Chapter 9
Living With the Inevitable 95

Taking Care of Business 96
Taxes Five Times a Year? 97
My Life as a Deduction 98

Chapter 10
The Secrets to Success. 101

The Skills and the Money 102
Building a Solid Foundation 103
The Company You'll Keep 103
Shut Down or Search On? 104

Appendix

Information Consultant Resources 105

Glossary 109

Index. 113

Preface

Want to be a professional know-it-all? Would you like to spend your days researching intriguing subjects, hunting down information, organizing presentations, and answering people's questions? If so, then read on, because this is definitely a book for you.

Given today's information explosion, fueled by hundreds of TV channels, the Internet, cell phones, satellite radio, broadband connections, e-mail, Wi-Fi , PDAs, pagers, voice mail, and the like, the most precious commodity of all is clearly information itself. But not just any old information. The information must be accurate, timely, and relevant to the person who needs it. It must be clear, concise, and cogent. It must be simple enough to understand and explain.

Enter the information consultant. A relatively recent phenomenon, the information consultant fills the enormous need in American life for a filter to sift through the data flooding us from all directions. In a time of ever-increasing content, the information consultant cuts through the clutter and finds what really matters, breaking down huge slabs of indigestible material into bite-sized chunks.

Some fantasists might even say that information consultants are our society's newest superheroes, caped crusaders battling the twin evils of information overload and distortion that threaten to overwhelm our ability to reason and our capacity to comprehend. After all, information consultants seek and defend the truth in a world filled with lies, innuendo, and half-truths. They pursue the actual facts in an age littered with assertions, opinions, and speculation. Certainly, it is rare to find an information consultant in red-and-blue tights, zooming through the air at supersonic speeds. The role played by information consultants is increasingly significant in business, medicine, technology, health care, employment, and other key areas. With new technologies promising to place even more information at our fingertips, the need to make sense of it all, or at least some part of it, will only become more pressing.

This book will show you how to be an information-age superhero. It will spell out the steps needed to become a consultant, start your own consulting practice, and build it into a thriving business. The book will explain who is best suited for this work, what tools you will need, where to look for the finest information, when to ask for help, how to attract clients, and why certain strategies work best.

We'll begin with an overview of the skills required for this kind of work and of the type of information that clients usually demand. Next we'll take you through a consultant's daily routine and the equipment and software you'll need. Then we'll focus on expenses, rates, and Internet search tips. Finally, we'll cover promotion, taxes, and specialization. Throughout the book, you'll hear from veteran information consultants who have built strong practices and wish to share the lessons they've learned.

Make sure you read every chapter because nearly all the material applies to every type of information consultant, no matter what specialty you may choose. Plus, the information is all interrelated.

Of course, reading this book can't guarantee that you'll be a great success at information consulting. Only your skills and drive, the market and, yes, a bit of luck will determine that. But if you read this book carefully, follow the steps outlined, and put in the effort required you stand a much better chance of succeeding.

So sit back in a comfy chair, take off your shoes and start thumbing through the pages. You, too, can be a professional know-it-all.

—Alan Breznick and Rachel Adelson

Becoming a
Know-It-All

Information consultant. It kind of sounds like someone James Bond would consult to find the location of stolen secret government documents, doesn't it? Bond slips you an envelope full of money, and you hand him a computer disk labeled "For Your Eyes Only," with all the information he so desperately needs but couldn't find himself. The country is saved, and you're off to the bank to make a deposit.

▲

While the real life of an information consultant may not have all the cloak-and-dagger stuff, who wouldn't trade that excitement for the ability to do all the sleuthing from the comfort of your own home—with the same trip to the bank at the end?

The Right Stuff

In the past, information consultants were generally ex-librarians or full-time librarians who moonlighted by doing extra research for clients. Things have changed a lot in the past 10 years. Now, primarily due to easier access to information online, information consultants can come from virtually any profession. Medical receptionists can become medical researchers. Magazine editors can become expert researchers in topics they used to cover in their magazines. Paralegals and legal secretaries can take their knowledge of legal matters into business, doing research for lawyers. It's even possible for you to become an information consultant without any experience in the field by subcontracting work from established consultants. The possibilities are endless.

Why, then, isn't everyone with any sense doing this type of work? The answer is simple: Many people are just not cut out for it. In the next section, we'll take a closer look at what it takes to be an information consultant, so you can decide whether the profession is right for you.

The Thrill of the Search

First off, if you're planning to become an information consultant because it sounds like easy money, forget it. While you may get lucky and find information for a client

---

Back to School

Learning the skills it takes to become an information consultant may sound like a lot of work. If you have the time and the money, however, it's entirely possible to get the training you need by hiring a mentor. A mentor is someone who already works in the field of information consulting and will—for a fee—teach you everything you need to know to enter the profession. Mentor programs usually take about a year to complete, but you walk away with a firm grasp of the skills necessary to become an information consultant. Another option is to attend a seminar on the specific field of research you intend to enter. Pricing for mentor programs and seminars varies widely. A good place to find a mentor or professional who gives seminars is The Association of Independent Information Professionals' membership listing on its Web site, www.aiip.org.

quickly every once in a while or find out that two clients want similar information, you'll have just as many jobs where you'll be pulling your hair out, trying to find information that doesn't seem to exist. The key to surviving in this field is to enjoy the work. Here are some questions you can ask yourself to help determine whether you're cut out for information consulting:

- *Do you like to read?* If so, that's a great start. As an information consultant, you'll spend a great amount of time reading magazine articles and Web pages that give you clues about the information you are looking for. You will frequently need to make the jump from being clueless on a subject to being an expert in just a few weeks. And that means hitting the books.

- *Do you like research?* It may well be that you've never spent large amounts of time looking for answers that others are willing to pay for. Try spending some time on the Internet and at the library to see if you really like doing research. Pick an obscure topic, maybe something you've read about in the nether regions of the newspaper, and try to find out absolutely everything you can about it. Sound like fun? Do you enjoy learning about things that you may not have ever thought to care about? If so, terrific! You've met yet another qualification. As an information consultant, you'll need to keep yourself interested in the matter at hand. Otherwise, every job will seem like working on a term paper in a class that you hate.

- *Are you a "people person"?* If you think being an information consultant will be your key to solitude or a means of escaping the rat race, you're in for a rude awakening. First of all, you need to be personable and confident enough to convincingly sell your services. You'll also frequently need to contact companies and experts to find the answers you're looking for. If you don't have excellent people skills, you're going to have real problems as an information consultant.

- *Are you a logical thinker?* Logical thinking is extremely important in this line of work. There's no master list of information that will magically appear for you to hand over to your client. You will need to make assumptions and educated guesses about where the information can be found, and these guesses will rarely be correct on the first try. You'll also need to help your clients pare their original requests down to the real nuts and bolts of what they're trying to find out. The narrower the focus, the more likely you are to find the information they need. Logical thinking is a big plus here; it's absolutely necessary for finding information on the Internet and in other formats.

Bright Idea

Even if you're not a librarian, most local libraries allow people to volunteer. Along with learning to dig through piles of printed materials, you'll probably pick up some new computer research skills. Most libraries are computerized, and most have access to the Internet and online databases.

- *Are you organized?* You better be. Strong organizational skills are necessary for running a business in general and for the specific tasks you'll undertake as an information consultant. You'll often be asked to take all the information you've gathered and turn it into a report that answers the questions your client needs to have addressed. For example, you might be required to present different factors your client needs to consider when making a particular business decision. You'll need to organize information as you acquire it, and then organize it again into logical chunks of information in which clients can clearly see the answers they're paying you for.

> **Smart Tip** Tip...
>
> You may already have some of the skills you'll need to be an information consultant and not even know it. Do you have good phone skills from doing telemarketing or a similar job? Are you particularly well organized when you call the bank with a question about your statement? You'll need to have a good phone presence and very specific questions when you're calling people for answers.

- *Are you disciplined?* Self-discipline is a prerequisite for all self-employed people. You need to set goals and follow through to accomplish them. The dream of deciding your own schedule is only true to a certain extent. What you'll really be doing is changing your schedule to meet the demands of your clients. Sure, you can take the occasional Friday afternoon off once in a while or work half a day, but your income will be directly related to what you put into your business in sweat. If you sleep in too often or miss deadlines, you'll lose clients—and income. The biggest lesson many self-employed people learn in their first year as business owners is that there are benefits to having a nine-to-five job with a salary.

- *Are you self-confident?* Every time you court a new client, it's like applying for a job. If you have trouble in situations like this, then being an information consultant is probably not right for you. Yes, you will gain confidence as you develop your business. But if applying for jobs is akin to jumping out of an airplane for you, ask yourself whether you can grow into this role. Remember, too, that you won't get every job you go after, and you'll have to accept rejection as par for the course.

- *Are you computer literate?* You don't have to learn how to program computers, but you do need to have a basic working knowledge of things like word processing programs, e-mail, and Internet searching. All of these are skills that can be acquired through practice or by taking classes. If the idea of sitting in front of a computer terminal for hours on end gives you the heebie-jeebies, you should know that most research is now done primarily through computers. Information consultants need to see the computer as a powerful and important research tool.

(Knowing how to type doesn't hurt, either. You'll have to deliver your information in a neat and readable format.)

- *Can you handle the financial demands of starting a new business?* You're probably not going to jump into this business and make a gigantic leap into financial prosperity. It pays well if you're good at it, but growing any business takes time. Do you have a nest egg in the bank that you can fall back on if you don't get any work for a few months? Does your spouse make enough money to cover the bills during slow periods? Have you discussed getting financial help from friends or relatives if business dies off for a while? Most information consultants will tell you that

> **⚠ Beware!**
> No matter how much you dislike the job you leave to become an information consultant, resist the temptation to give your boss a piece of your mind on your way out the door. This is especially important if you work for a company that might be able to use your services in the future. As we've said, the company you leave may be your first client. Don't burn any bridges!

you'll have financial ups and downs. Some of this is due to cycles in particular areas of research. If you do high-tech research for software companies, for example, many of them slow to almost a complete stop during the holiday season. After a year or so, you'll have a better idea about when your busy and slow times will be, and the money you make when you're busy will carry you through the slow periods. Just be financially prepared to pay your bills—one way or another—if you have a few slow months. (For more information about financing your business, see Chapter 4, "Getting Financing," in *Start-Up Basics*.)

While all of these skills are important, they can all be developed over time. If you have most of them developed, and you think you'll enjoy this sort of work, then go for it. If being an information consultant sounds great, but you're missing these important skills, take some time to develop them before jumping in. Take some computer classes if that's what you need to do. Remember, it's also possible to start out slow, working part-time as an information consultant while keeping your current job.

Finding Your Area of Expertise

Most information consultants start their businesses by doing work in fields they already have some experience in. As we mentioned earlier, people involved in the legal profession frequently start their businesses by doing research for law firms, and those involved in medicine often start off doing medical research. We all have to start somewhere, and beginning with something in which you already have a background can be a big plus. Many people even leave their jobs (on good terms, of course) and start their businesses with their ex-employer as their first client.

The Road Less Traveled

Information consultants come from all walks of life. How they get into the business is a mystery to outsiders but makes perfect sense once you see the chain of events in their lives. One information consultant who does medical research told us her story. "I have a long history of medical conditions in my family, and we've always had to rely on doctors to tell us what to do. I have a medical background—I was a medical technologist, and I did market research about medical products. When I found out that there was online information available, I thought, 'This is something I could have used many times in my life,' so I wanted to help other people get access to it."

Another consultant, Derek P., a former vice president of business development for a multinational corporation, who is based in Caledon East, Ontario, explains, "I had business experience using online databases for acquisition work with a company I was employed by, and prior to that, I had used them for market research. I've been using them since the late '70s. When the company was taken over, I decided to use these skills and my business background to get me started."

Two completely different backgrounds, one common profession—information consultant.

If you don't think you have an area of expertise, do a little research. You'll be surprised at the variety and extent of the information that companies need. Take a look at the Web sites for organizations devoted to information professionals. A good one to check out is The Association of Independent Information Professionals' Web site, www.aiip.org. There you can look at a list of AIIP members and the type of work they do. Many organizations like the AIIP have Web sites that also feature links to their members' sites. A look at the membership lists of these professional organizations and a quick visit to some of their members' sites will show you that information professionals specialize in everything from arts and humanities to zoology.

Do a little more searching, and you'll find that organizations such as the AIIP will allow you to join as an associate member. The AIIP offers a mentor program free to members, where you can get advice about starting and operating your business from seasoned professionals. It could be a good place to get started. The organization also has a referral program for members.

Don't be discouraged by the fact that you will probably start out doing research in the field you used to work in. Over the course of time, through an almost illogical series of events, most information consultants end up doing research in more than one field—including a few they never thought they would be involved in. How does this happen? Let's say an editor for a computer-aided drafting magazine starts his information consulting business doing research on engineering and architecture design tools for his former employer. In the same building is a magazine devoted to computer animation and 3-D design, which hires him because its director has heard he does good work. He does research on tools for animators (which they are happy with), and they give him another assignment: putting together a listing of big-time movie animation and special-effects studios. The next thing he knows, he gets a call from a Hollywood movie studio asking for his services in locating special-effects studios that are appropriate for movies they are working on. From engineering to Hollywood, in three easy (well, maybe not exactly easy) steps.

Stat Fact

The *Burwell World Directory of Information Brokers* and The Association of Independent Information Professionals each list fewer than 1,000 people worldwide. Even if there are twice that many information professionals currently working in the field, it only amounts to the population of a couple of big-city high schools. Certainly, there's plenty of room for more information consultants in the Information Age.

Who's in the Market for Information?

In decades past, information consultants were considered dealers in obscure information. Companies hired them to dig through those dusty old libraries and spools of microfiche to locate information that was difficult or too costly in terms of personnel hours to locate. Times have sure changed. Such a huge amount of information is now available that those who hire information consultants are often paying to have the information narrowed down to a few key topics. For example, a search for the phrase "Information Broker" on a popular search engine brings up no fewer than 33,000 listings! If the Web keeps expanding as it has in the past ten years, it won't be long before clients start hiring information consultants to find other information consultants (just kidding, but you get the idea). So much information is available that those trying to find it can't see the forest for the trees. The talent shared by those who pursue information consulting as their life's work is the ability to enter that same forest and return in a reasonable amount of time with a list of the location and size of all the pine trees.

Filtering information has become such a big business that in some areas—especially the fast-moving, high-tech world—there's a large market for specialized information. In these areas, some consultants make their living by researching specific topics and offering their findings for sale on the Web. They use the information itself to attract customers. Some even collect data on specific industries and charge customers a subscription fee to receive weekly bulletins via e-mail.

Many companies do not have the resources to do their own research. They may also not need research done regularly enough to justify taking on an employee to perform it. It is generally far more expensive to hire an employee and provide the needed equipment and benefits than it is to hire outside help. Here are a few of the types of clients you can expect to work for, should you decide information consulting is for you:

Bright Idea

Virtually every industry needs information consultants at some point. If you are still working at another job, finding out whether your company hires people for outside research is a good way to get ideas about how you might start out on the road to becoming an information consultant. Who knows? Your current employer may even become one of your first clients.

- *Lawyers looking for the historical background of a particular type of case:* Attorneys constantly need to sort through old lawsuits to find precedent-setting decisions. Smaller firms are more likely to need outside help with this task. This type of information consulting is particularly fitting if you have a background in law—if you've been a paralegal or worked in the research department of a large legal firm, for example.

- *Corporations looking for information on competitors and potential suppliers:* Believe it or not, many large companies really aren't all that knowledgeable about their competitors. Some will hire you to find out everything from the specifics of another company's product line to figures that show how profitable a rival company has been over the past few years. Some use this information to make sure they remain competitive, and others use it to scope out potential strategic partners, suppliers, and even companies to buy.

- *Companies or individuals looking for patent information:* There's no reason to reinvent the wheel, right? That's why many companies hire information consultants to find out about potential patent and ownership conflicts. This is an especially important subject for high-tech developers, whose ideas may be considered intellectual property even if they're not patented.

- *Magazines compiling buyer's guides:* If you've ever seen a 50-page buyer's guide in a magazine, chances are it was put together by an information consultant. Most publications don't have the time or the resources to put together a complete listing of products and services for their readers. This can be a good place to start for information consultants with knowledge of a particular industry.

- *Publishing companies looking for untapped markets in hopes of starting new magazines or newsletters:* Publishing companies, especially ones that publish several magazines that each serve niche markets with small numbers of subscribers, are constantly trying to identify new markets. Once a new market is found, the search for competitors begins (to be sure there is a need for a new publication), and research is conducted to find out whether the market is valuable enough to warrant launching a new publication.

- *Investors seeking company background information:* Sometimes the stock market numbers don't give the entire story. So providing financial and historical data on companies can help investors decide where to spend their money.

What's That Information Worth?

The information consulting business is generally a one-person operation, though it is certainly possible to expand and take on employees. The fact that it's a business you can start from home means you can get started for a relatively small amount of money (between $5,000 and $7,000). And depending on your expertise, you can gross anywhere from $35,000 to $100,000 per year working full time.

What Do You Need to Get Started?

First, you need to work well on your own. Clients won't be paying you to spend the day in the park and, while working at home does give many a newfound sense of freedom, companies expect you to meet deadlines. Whether you need to work nights and weekends to meet their deadlines is not their problem.

Second, you will need a working knowledge of computers—especially when searching the Internet. Many people already have a basic knowledge of computers, but if you don't, it would be worthwhile to take a few classes.

Keep in mind that the computer will not be your only source of information. You'll still need to make phone calls to check information, conduct interviews, and just ask questions. Interpersonal skills are a big plus. And, yes, you'll sometimes need to make a trip to the library or the bookstore, or get out of the house to meet with clients, so you won't be totally isolated.

The Tools at Your Disposal

Finding information for clients is like solving a mystery. And today, information consultants have more high-tech tools for research, marketing, and sales at their disposal than ever before. The wealth of information on the World Wide Web gives you a tremendous head start over those who undertook this business in decades past. Before the introduction of the Web, most research done by information consultants began in a library, with the

Fun Fact

By most accounts, the profession of information consulting (by individuals who aren't librarians or corporate researchers) was started by Sue Rugge in 1971, making it a field just more than 30 years old. Getting started in the business right now means you'll still be part of a new and exciting industry.

tedious task of sifting through reference books, piles of magazines, or microfiche for clues. These days, the first place information consultants look is usually the World Wide Web, which features information on everything from company contacts and articles from back issues of magazines, to financial disclosures made to the U.S. government by the largest public corporations in the country. To make things even more appealing, the information provided comes not just from the United States but from the entire world.

The Net offers billions of pages of information on nearly every topic imaginable. The U.S. government alone maintains more than 12,519 sites, which contain a variety of information that includes corporate annual reports, patent listings, and much more. This is just the beginning for information consultants, who can use the Web to track down listings of contact information, books, periodicals, and other reference materials.

Beware!

Because most research is done in front of a computer, try testing yourself by researching a few topics on your own. Many people simply have a lot of trouble sitting in front of that glowing, humming box for long periods of time—something you don't want to discover a few weeks after going into business as an information consultant.

2

Background Check
The Information Market

Just about any type of business you can imag-
ine has a need for information. Regardless of your field of
interest or expertise, it's almost a sure bet that someone
somewhere is willing to pay for your services. This chapter will
give you an overview of the types of information that people
are looking for. It is intended to help get those wheels in your

head turning in your effort to find a market, as well as give you a head start on identifying your competition.

Who Needs Information, and Why?

If you have ever worked as a librarian or a researcher for a large company, you already know the value of information. If you're just getting started or you're reading this guide to see what the business is all about, here are some examples of the types of companies and individuals that might use the services of an information consultant.

Corporations Assessing Competition

Corporations need to know what's going on in their industries so they can stay competitive. However, they may not have the resources or the know-how to locate all the information they need. For example, if a large electronics company (we'll call it Titan Electronics) is considering introducing a new type of audio system, it may hire an information consultant to gather information about what its competitors are doing. Here are some of the questions Titan Electronics might want answered:

- *Who is the competition?* This one may sound a little silly, but large companies often don't have much information about smaller, more specialized companies or about the announcements of known competitors. Maybe there's a start-up in Boise, Idaho, that has a lot of investment capital and plans to introduce a single targeted product that's of a higher quality, or will be earlier to market than Titan Electronics' product. Maybe ten such companies exist. Maybe Titan missed an announcement from its biggest rival or an article about new technology. Maybe the company missed a review calling a competitor's product the best thing since sliced bread or the worst thing since a stubbed toe.

- *How successful is the competition?* Companies frequently need to track down financial information about competitors, including bits of information that may not show up on NASDAQ or NYSE. Did any of their competitors recently change CEOs? Have they recently moved into new facilities? Have they increased their workforce? Have they announced alliances or mergers that may help them compete with Titan Electronics?

> **Beware!**
> Many information consultants end up doing work for more than one client in the same industry—sometimes even competitors. The work you do for each client must be kept confidential. Failure to keep a client's confidentiality will not only ruin your reputation but also sour the client to other information consultants. It can also result in legal action from the company whose secrets you shared.

- *What are the risk factors in introducing this new product?* Corporations may also need to know what the financial climate is in their industry. Was there a hurricane in the home country of their widget supplier? Historically, how successful have other companies been in introducing radical new home audio technology that they hope will displace everything else on the market? How healthy is the home electronics industry overall? Has the economy affected consumers' buying power?

Corporations Preparing for Buyouts or Mergers

Corporations that are looking to buy or merge with companies that produce competing or complementary products need a substantial amount of information. They would, for example, have to investigate the financial pros and cons of merging with a competitor or purchasing a supplier. Depending on your client's needs, this type of information consulting can be tricky. You may be asked to find this information without contacting the companies you are gathering information about, or without telling anyone who your client is.

Companies That Need Product Information

This area of research varies widely. It includes finding information on specific types of software applications that companies will be investing in, computer hardware and software prices and capabilities, and even ergonomic factors that may arise from purchasing specific types of office furniture. While this type of information may seem trivial, companies that are purchasing a 100-seat license of a certain software application or 1,000 chairs often hire information consultants to help them make the right purchasing decisions.

Companies That Need Medical Information

Medical information consulting takes many forms. As in any corporation, medical supply and pharmaceutical companies have to keep on top of their industries to remain competitive. Is there a market for a particular type of drug or medical device? Are other businesses in the market turning a profit from the proposed product? Is there room in the market for additional companies to make a profit selling similar products? These questions are similar to those asked by corporations assessing their competition.

Individuals Researching Medical Conditions

One information consultant we spoke with does research for individuals about the type of medical treatment they are receiving and alternative treatments. Despite our reverence for doctors, most of them (especially the good ones) will admit that they don't know everything. In addition to getting a second opinion, presenting doctors with information about the illness that has been diagnosed, or information about other possible diagnoses, can help people get better medical treatment. This area of research should not be entered into lightly, and you'll want to have a lawyer help you draw up contracts that limit your liability.

Individuals Looking for Personal Information

For reasons that range from checking the truth of someone's resume to locating a long-lost relative, people often want to find personal information about other people. This type of research is performed for clients that include lawyers, private investigators, employers, and even people digging into the pasts of potential spouses. Researching personal backgrounds is not for the faint of heart. While the information you are providing to the client is generally available in public records, there's no guarantee that the client's intentions are honorable. Before you start conducting personal research for clients, be sure to talk to a lawyer about potential liabilities. (For more information about hiring a lawyer, check out Chapter 7, "Business Insurance," in *Start-Up Basics*.)

If you're interested in becoming a seeker of information about individuals, you can hone your skills by trying to locate information about old friends you've lost track of, or about a celebrity you admire. Just about everybody has a phone number and an e-mail address nowadays, so a good place to start is the White Pages Web site at www.whitepages.com, which includes "Find a Person" and "Find a Business" subsites. Two other useful sites are www.411.com and www.infobel.com/teldir, which search phone numbers worldwide.

Finding a Market for Your Services

Reading the examples of the different types of information that people and companies are willing to pay for may lead you to wonder if there's anyone who doesn't need the services of an information consultant. The fact of the matter is, just about anyone can benefit from having more information. As the old saying goes, Knowledge is power.

As an information consultant trying to make a living, you'll need to find out not only who needs information, but also who has the financial resources to pay for it. Hopefully, the suggestions

Smart Tip

Following trends in the industry you hope to serve and in related industries can give you a clue as to where the money lies. Keep an eye on the stock market, and faithfully read the business sections of magazines to see which types of companies are flourishing. These are also the industries that will have the most need for information consultants to keep their businesses competitive.

given in this chapter will get the old gears turning in your head. If you have a background in general research or library science, you've got a head start into just about any area of research. If not, it's probably a good idea to keep your focus fairly narrow when you're starting out. Ask yourself these questions:

- What subject would you be considered an authority on?
- Is there a need for research in this area?
- Are you willing to spend some time upfront to find out whether those who need the information you can provide will actually pay for research?
- Is there a related field that may be more lucrative that you could learn more about?

All of these questions are important. If you intend to support yourself as an information consultant, you need to find paying customers. Unfortunately, the areas that information consultants serve are very diverse, which makes it difficult to describe the actual procedures you'll use to find out whether there is a need for your talents.

Right on Target

While most information consultants will tell you that you need to target a particular niche market, how you find clients may have more to do with your ability to find a market and adapt your services to it than with your expertise in a particular subject.

For Stephanie A., an information consultant in Wilmington, Delaware, a degree in library science definitely made her more adaptable. "I remember going to my first conference of information consultants and hearing one of the founders of the organization say that you have to have a 'niche.' I remember saying to myself, 'Why?' You really don't know what area is going to be hot. At the time, I was concentrating on industries I thought understood information and were willing to pay for it, rather than looking for a particular subject area. I targeted publishers because I had been in charge of publisher relations at my previous company. I had a lot of contacts in that field, and I knew that publishers who were putting together books, indexes, and journals had a thirst for information and certainly could afford it."

Stephanie has since adapted to providing information in a completely different field. "Each year it's a little bit different. For the last couple of years, the pharmaceutical industry has paid most of the bills," she says. "I think it's another group that has a tremendous amount of money to spend on information. They understand it, they appreciate it, and they're willing to pay just about anything for it."

▲

Smart Tip

Tip...

Use your knowledge to become a resource within the community of information consultants. Even being an expert on computers and other important tools of the trade can be useful to others. Who knows? Maybe someone will be offered work by a computer manufacturer and use you as a subcontractor based on your understanding of the nuts and bolts of computing.

A good first step is to become a voracious reader. Read absolutely every magazine and book that is available about your subject of choice. Become an expert. Becoming an expert on a particular subject is not as difficult as it sounds. That's because most people are too busy doing their jobs to really learn everything there is to know about the field in which they work.

Once you've picked an area of expertise, test your research skills by finding contacts at companies you can provide services for. Call them up and introduce yourself. If they've never hired an information consultant, just knowing that someone is available may entice them to use your services. As you engage in this little exercise, you may be surprised by the number of companies that enlist the aid of information consultants.

Another way to find out more about the market for information in your area of expertise is to join an organization such as the AIIP (The Association of Independent Information Professionals, remember?). This kind of organization gives you access to people who have years of experience as information consultants. The AIIP also provides a members-only listing on the Internet where you can display your area of expertise and find others who do similar types of research. The *Annual Membership Directory* is free to members, $75 to nonmembers, and the referral program is free to members, providing up to three names of members who may be able to help (though they'll do actual work only for a fee). The key to taking advantage of this type of resource is to become a resource yourself. You may need information on starting a business, and someone else may ask your advice on issues in your area of strength. You'll reap as much as you sow.

Established information consultants rarely turn down a job—even if it isn't in their particular knowledge niche. It's entirely possible that another consultant may hire you as a subcontractor, based on your background or skill set. While the client may not know who you are, it's a foot in the door and a great way to get experience. (For more information on market research, see Chapter 1, "Conducting Market Research," in *Start-Up Basics*.)

Identifying the Competition

An important part of any decision to start a business is deciding whether there is room in the market for your type of services. Most of the information consultants and experts we interviewed have described the field of information consulting as one of mutual support among those in the profession. Rather than competing with each other for jobs, most consultants see other information consultants as resources. This sort of altruism makes the field of information consulting all the more attractive.

The *Information Broker's Handbook*, an excellent book by Sue Rugge and Alfred Glossbrenner, even goes as far as saying that an information consultant should never turn down a job, even if it's not within his or her field of expertise. Instead, consultants should

Smart Tip
Respect the experts and learn from them. If you know of an information consultant who is better versed in a subject than you are, hiring him or her as a subcontractor will help you earn while you learn.

accept the work and seek out other information consultants who are more familiar with the subject matter, either for advice, paid consulting, or paid subcontracting. This is not to say that information consultants never compete with each other for work. Competition does exist—in some cases, where you'd least expect it. But it's definitely not in your best interest to burn bridges with other consultants or use business practices that will alienate you from others in the profession.

The Information Explosion

With the massive amount of information on the Internet today, many companies have come to the false conclusion that information consultants just aren't necessary anymore. If they're looking for small amounts of information or happen to get lucky a couple of times and find what they're looking for, this conclusion is further fortified. Fear not, brave consultant. The first time these companies spend a week's worth of time looking for a needle in a haystack that you could find in a day or two, your value will be proven. It takes a lot of expertise, practice, and sometimes training to find needles in haystacks, whether the haystack is the Internet or another type of online database.

If you use online databases such as Dialog, you'll either have to become proficient at using the Internet or find someone who is, so that you can subcontract work to them. Why? The media has given many people the idea that absolutely every bit of information in the universe is now available for little more than a monthly fee to an Internet service provider (ISP). Because many other online databases charge (sometimes very high rates) for access time, many clients seeking information request that a certain number of hours be spent sifting through the Net. That's because they want to see if what they need is available without the added expense of hourly online database rates.

The Kindly (and Free) Librarian

Before information consulting came on the scene some 30 years ago, research was done mostly at libraries, where the friendly folks behind the reference desk could help people find the information they needed at no charge. This has changed considerably over the years. Most libraries across the United States have cut their staffs to the point where there is no longer anyone behind the reference desk to answer questions. In fact, many ex-librarians become information consultants either due to job cuts or because it's simply more lucrative. As library staffs have shrunk due to budget cuts and other factors, the competition information consultants face from librarians has significantly decreased.

Inhouse Research Staffs

Many large corporations have their own staffs of information professionals for research projects, but this doesn't necessarily take you out of the loop for getting work. Why? Confidentiality, for one. For more sensitive research, companies will sometimes farm out jobs to independent information professionals to keep certain research from leaking out through company gossip. Nobody wants an acquisition or merger plan ruined by gossip around the water cooler or a happy-hour conversation overheard by a bartender whose spouse works for the competition's lawyers.

At least one information consultant we talked to, Stephanie A., whose business is based in Wilmington, Delaware, had actually done such a good job for a company that it decided to hire its own inhouse research staff. Talk about irony! This isn't actually as ugly as it sounds. An information consultant in this situation could still be hired for confidential projects or could even get a referral from that client to another company. So don't worry about doing too good a job.

Playing the Field

Companies that have hired and been happy with more than one information consultant in the past will occasionally get you to compete with another consultant without your knowledge. In other words, they call up two consultants to get bids without telling the consultants that they are taking more than one bid. Then they call up the more expensive consultant and tell him or her that the other has bid a lower rate. This situation can lead to misunderstandings and bad feelings, but sometimes it can't be avoided. Yet another good reason to belong to a professional association: If the consultant who won the bid is on your association's roster, it makes it that much easier to clear up any misunderstandings. After all, if you were both bidding on the same job, you are probably both specializing in the same field and your paths may cross again in the future.

The more you look into the market, the clearer it becomes that information is valuable to any business, proving that there's room in the market for your services. Once businesses realize the power of information and see that there are professionals who can supply what they need, they will grasp that it is not something they should undertake on their own. Just because you understand in a general way how brain surgery works, doesn't mean you're going to try it. As businesses are exposed to the glut of information available, they will see that it takes a trained professional to separate the wheat from the chaff.

FAQs

Now that you have a better idea about the markets that information consultants serve, let's work on answering some of the other questions you must be asking yourself by now. What's life really like as an information consultant? How will you structure your business? Will you need to hire employees? Where will you set up shop? This chapter takes a look at the ins and outs of being an information consultant and explores the decisions you'll need to make as you lay the foundation for your business. We'll discuss everything from the average workday to naming your business and choosing a location for your office. In the field of information consulting, nearly all the details of doing business are variables. Take a look at your options, and try to figure out what you will be comfortable with.

A Day in the Life

What can you expect to deal with each day as an information consultant? Well, as with any job, each day will bring its own challenges and rewards. When you're self-employed, as most information consultants are, discipline is required on a daily basis. You'll only be "making your own schedule" as far as your projects will allow. Sure, you may have a few days or afternoons when you can take a little time off, but you'll more than likely spend those downtimes drumming up business—unless you're so far ahead financially that you can afford to nap in the hammock for a while.

In this section, we'll take a look at a typical day in the life of an information consultant. This little synopsis assumes you're taking on the entire consulting business on your own. If you're going to be working with another person who takes on some of these tasks, you'll have more time to spend on your portion of the work—but you'll also need to get enough work to support the two (or more) of you.

9:00 A.M. Check Your E-Mail and Phone Messages

E-mail is the communication method of choice in today's business world. You'll need to check your e-mail constantly throughout the day for messages from clients. It's a good, quick way to send off brief notes, questions, and project updates. Because it's difficult to convey attitudes such as sarcasm via e-mail, keep your messages as businesslike as possible to avoid misunderstandings. E-mail is frequently forwarded to others by those who receive it—sometimes to co-workers and sometimes to superiors to keep them updated on the status of a project. This is yet another reason for brevity and professionalism.

One of the many advantages of e-mail is that it allows you to keep a record of the correspondence you have with clients. With a little software savvy, you can create for yourself

> **Smart Tip**
>
> Try to pay attention to the time of day you're best able to do certain tasks. For example, you may not feel like making phone calls right when you start working, and may prefer instead to concentrate on research over your morning cup of coffee. You're the boss, and (within normal constraints) you can decide what time of day to take care of what.

an electronic paper trail that shows what was requested by whom. Many e-mail programs will even sort your messages into different folders as they come in, so that you can keep the correspondence you have with each client separate.

Check your phone messages next. If you are on the West Coast, clients in the eastern part of the country have a three-hour head start on you (unless you're a really early riser) and may already have been waiting a few hours for the answer to a question by the time you're having your morning cup of coffee. Follow up on any calls you've received from clients about current and future work—especially future work. When you're first starting out, it's quite possible to miss getting a job by not responding fast enough.

9:30 A.M. Primary Research

Unless a client specifically asks only for what you can find on the Web or another online resource, you're going to have to do some primary research to fill out what you've dug up electronically—or from libraries or wherever else you've been researching. Primary research means going straight to the horse's mouth by calling companies or people who have written articles about the topic you're researching.

Your client may want information about a company's size, correct address, number of years in business, or other tidbits that may be missing from the places you've investigated. While you're conducting primary research to find the answers to these questions,

---

Delicate Delegating

The number of tasks you'll need to accomplish as an information consultant may seem daunting, but knowing which duties can be delegated to others can help you keep your business running smoothly. The question you always need to ask yourself is: "Do I have more time, or do I have more money?"

If you're making gobs of money, why not spend a little extra so you can concentrate on your main job instead of all the peripheral tasks that need to be taken care of to run your business? You can hire an accountant to take care of your quarterly and annual taxes, or a bookkeeper to track your income and expenses. You can hire someone part-time to take care of billing and paperwork, or pay someone to edit and format reports you've gathered information for. You can have someone transcribe tapes of interviews with experts or even give your child or a neighbor's a couple of bucks to go to the post office for you.

The more time you spend being an information consultant rather than your own bookkeeper, accountant, administrative staff, and billing department, the more money you'll make. If business is slow, do it all yourself. But if business is good, cut yourself some slack and let someone else do the small stuff.

Beware!

"Make hay while the sun shines" is an old saying among farmers that translates to "work first, play later" for information consultants. Avoid the temptation to put off work until you get close to a deadline. If you figure a job will take three days and the deadline isn't for a couple of weeks, get started on it early. Little things like computer problems, illness, or even a power outage can lay waste to the best-laid plans.

be careful not to misrepresent yourself or betray any confidentiality agreement you have with your client. For some projects—for example, a company gathering information about the price of medical tools it is interested in buying—the confidentiality issue won't pose much of a problem because the company you're calling may actually profit from giving you the information. Just be sure you're clear about whether your client company wants its identity exposed.

Primary research frequently involves interviewing experts about a subject. You'll need to find these experts first, but they can be very helpful in keeping you up-to-date. If you're focusing on a particular area of research, developing good relationships with experts can be very valuable. Are there magazines or newsletters devoted to your area of expertise? Subscribe to them, and try to develop relationships with the editors. Are there conferences devoted to your research specialty? Attend them (cost permitting) to keep up-to-date on new developments and make other important contacts.

11:00 A.M. Contracts, Bills, Invoices, and Project Scheduling

Ahh, here we are. The inevitable (and usually least favorite) part of running any business: paperwork. Establishing contracts with clients is important; it ensures that both you and the client know what to expect. Is there a limit to the number of hours you'll work? Are there limits to where you'll do the research? Maybe the client doesn't want you to call vendors directly. Perhaps the client doesn't want you to use more expensive online services like Dialog. Is it clear how much you'll be charging for the job? All these things need to be reviewed carefully and put in writing to prevent you and the client from having misunderstandings later in the research process. While not all the information consultants we spoke to draw up contracts for their clients, those who have been burned by not having the parameters of a project clearly defined on paper swear by them.

Because every type of research is different, and clients all have different needs and requirements, there is really no standard contract. For example, in some market research, liability isn't much of a problem; but in medical or legal research, it can be a real danger (e.g., someone dies or loses a legal case because your work was not good enough). Contracts are generally hammered out with the client. It's a good idea to run your contract by a lawyer if you're worried about potential liability.

Pay the bills. You don't want your phone shut off in the middle of a project, and you don't want your ISP to cut off your Internet access. Have you subcontracted any work to other information consultants? If so, pay them promptly, just as you would expect a client to pay you. Are any of your clients late in paying you? Give them a call after 30 days to check on the status of your payment. Have you sent out invoices for the work you've completed? The longer you wait to send out an invoice, the longer it will take you to get paid. Have you paid for your magazine and newsletter subscriptions? Have you tracked all this information so you can pay the required quarterly income tax installments? If not, you have some work to do.

> **⚠ Beware!**
> All work and no play does indeed make Jack a dull boy. Try to stay in contact with the outside world to keep yourself inspired, and exchange ideas with others. Whether you join a professional organization or just make time to "do lunch" once in a while with someone who does the same type of work you do, the opportunity to "talk shop" will give you tips you can use to make your business more successful.

Check your schedule to make sure you know what your workload is going to be like in the next month or two. Too much or too little work can be equally damaging to your business. To avoid financially devastating downtime, you need to make time to find work even when you're in the middle of a project. Make sure you set aside time for this no matter how busy you are, especially when you're starting out. Famine can quickly follow feast. Remember, it may take you a month to get paid for that gigantic job that kept you from scrounging around for work. This is why it's really important to keep an eye on your billing and scheduling. You want as steady a flow of income as possible. It takes some time to get the rhythm down, but you'll figure it out.

Believe it or not, having too much work can also be a problem. In time, you'll establish relationships with other information consultants to whom you can subcontract work. Until then, if you overburden yourself, you will be doing your clients a disservice by not putting the amount of effort they expect into their projects. Worse, you may miss important deadlines that affect their businesses. Either way, it's unlikely they'll give you a second chance. Overloading yourself may make you a big chunk of money fast, but it can damage your business in the future.

12:00 P.M. Lunch?

OK, go ahead and raid the refrigerator. You may want to take this opportunity to review the status of projects you'll be tearing into after lunch or to read the industry magazines and newsletters you subscribe to. You'll have to make time for these tasks at some point during the day, so you might as well do your reading and eating in the kitchen to keep the crumbs out of your keyboard.

12:30 P.M. Start Searching!

Finding information is your business. Spend the next two hours online, whether it's on the Internet or one of the commercial online databases. You'll become more proficient at deciding which one to use as time goes on and you develop better intuition about where to find information. You'll also realize it much earlier when you've spent too much time on a wild-goose chase. Sometimes you can gain more information by making a single phone call than from spending hours online. Make a list of calls to make tomorrow.

2:30 P.M. Errands

Do you need to copy documents? Go to the post office to mail invoices and/or contracts? Are there any urgent packages to send by FedEx? Do you have blank cassettes for interviews? Ink and paper for your printer? Make a quick run to take care of these tasks.

3:30 P.M. Search Some More

After getting out for a little fresh air on your way to the post office, etc., your eyes will be a little less bleary than they were when you left. Back to work! Find that information!

5:00 P.M. Organize

Spend the next half-hour backing up any work you've done using your method of choice. If you wake up in the morning to find that your computer won't start, at least you'll have the data in some form (such as on disk or tape). The only thing worse than a hard-drive crash is losing information you've worked hard on. While this kind of catastrophe may only happen to you once or twice in your whole career (or maybe never), it's not worth losing clients over. Now spend some time organizing the piles of printed material you've generated during the course of the day.

5:30 P.M. Miller Time!

Time to sit back and sip your brew of choice? Maybe, but not necessarily. There are a number of things we haven't fit into our day:

- Phone calls can come in at any time, delaying your other daily activities.
- Meetings with clients can easily eat up half a day.
- Trips to the library can set you back a few hours but are sometimes necessary.
- Quarterly taxes will take a day out of your schedule four times a year.
- Emergency rush jobs may come up. (These often pay well, but don't let them ruin jobs you're doing for other clients.)
- Marketing, in whatever form you choose (mailings, maintaining a Web page, and so on), must be done.

- Making yourself more visible by writing articles or speaking at conferences can take up considerable time.
- The information you've gathered for your clients has to be formatted into a readable report.

All this, of course, is assuming you're working full-time as an information consultant. It's possible to get started in this profession working part-time or just in the evenings (though it can make contacting clients a little tricky). You can also partner with someone who has complementary skills, or subcontract work to other information consultants. But as a full-time information consultant, you need to keep all the balls in the air at once.

The schedule set forth here is only intended to show you the tasks you'll need to get accomplished—one way or another. Your daily schedule is something you'll develop over time. The thing to remember is that your clients are hiring you to keep their schedules, and the occasional night or weekend spent working is almost inevitable. However, as a self-employed person, it works the other way as well. When you're far enough ahead financially and have work scheduled for the future, there's no boss checking to see whether you're sitting in your cubicle. Reward yourself by sleeping in or doing something fun while the rest of corporate America is sitting in traffic on the way to work. Just pick an appropriate time for this kind of rebellious behavior, and don't let your business suffer for it.

> **Tip...**
>
> **Smart Tip**
> Running out of essentials like paper and printer cartridges can cause you a big delay, especially if it happens after the office supply store closes. Buying in bulk—say a case of paper instead of a ream, or a package of five ink cartridges instead of one—is not only good insurance but can also save you money. Better yet, you can also save time by ordering supplies online; some retailers (such as Staples .com) offer free shipping for orders above a certain amount.

Structuring Your Business

When you start doing business as an information consultant, you will more than likely fall under the heading of sole proprietorship. The truth is, the vast majority of those in your field continue to do business as sole proprietorships throughout their careers. In this section, we'll take a look at some of the options you'll have when you hit the big leagues. Chapter 2, *"Business Structure,"* in *Start-Up Basics* will give you a good overview of the different types of business structures you may want to consider as your business grows and becomes more successful.

There's a basic philosophical question that you should consider before deciding to take on the world with a cutting-edge company whose team of employees is available to provide every kind of information under the sun. Many consultants who have been in the business long enough to have lots of clients and steady work find that they make enough money staying independent. Once you become an expert, you may find that you value having only yourself to supervise and being wholly responsible for your own success.

Teaming Up

As an independent information consultant, you have to wear many hats. You do your own marketing, advertising, telephone research, library research, and online research—all this along with estimating costs and meeting with clients to help them figure out what they need to know. It may well be that you don't excel at some of these tasks or just plain don't like to do them. Why not start a partnership with someone who has complementary skills? It's not uncommon for an information consultant to be great at gathering information online but lousy at communicating with clients or interviewing people on the phone. It's also not uncommon for someone to be great at doing work but not so great at finding work. Perhaps your spouse or another immediate family member has the skills you lack? There are distinct tax advantages to hiring family members, some of which are mentioned in Chapter 6, "Employees, Benefits, and Policies," in *Start-Up Basics*.

Subcontracting

If you find that you have too many projects to handle at one time, you can pay other consultants to do the work for you. In general, the people you subcontract work to should be people whose skills you're confident about but who charge less per hour than you do. After you've gained enough experience to accurately estimate what to charge clients for your services, the advice of many information consultants is never to turn down a job (assuming that you're satisfied with the bid and confident that the client will pay you). In theory, if you're good at the marketing end of things, you can make your living bidding jobs and subcontracting the work to others. In fact, many information consultants have a certain aspect of the work that they don't like and, once they have enough clients, they are more than happy to pay someone else to do the dirty work.

Make sure you ask your subcontractor for a bid before you make a bid to a client, so that you can prepare it in a way that will allow you to pay the subcontractor and still keep a slice of the pie for yourself. When you hire a subcontractor, you will still be the client's contact person and you'll be responsible for explaining exactly what you (and your client) need from that subcontractor. Also keep in mind that, from the

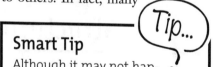

Smart Tip

Although it may not happen often, you can subcontract to people who make more money than you do. Just make sure you mark up the price to the client enough that you get a piece of the action, too. After all, the client contacted you, so you've saved the other consultant the trouble of finding work.

subcontractor's point of view, you are the client, and you're expected to pay for the sub-contractor's services in a timely manner—whether or not your client pays you right away.

There are also tax regulations that you need to keep in mind when subcontracting work to others. As long as the person doing the work is a contractor and not your employee, you are not responsible for sending a cut of his or her pay to the government as income tax. However, you are required to file a form 1099 with the IRS for any contractor whom you paid more than $600, and you must send a copy of the form to the contractor. It's also a good idea to have a written agreement with the information consultant to whom you are subcontracting work, one that specifies that the person is indeed an independent contractor. You don't want any trouble with the IRS. You should also check your state's laws to find out whether you need to report the payment to them as well. A good accountant will come in handy here.

Big, Bigger, Biggest

Information consulting firms traditionally include one to five people—usually one. That doesn't mean it's impossible to start a larger company, just that in the past it has been rare. The increased demand for information, and the frustration of companies and individuals who know it's out there but can't get to it themselves, means that the market for larger information companies is now ripe. Information consulting presents a potentially lucrative business opportunity for a group of people with the appropriate skills. Pooling resources with others might allow consultants to provide services that complement each other to the extent that it would make financial sense to consolidate into a larger company. Getting consultants with complementary skills to work together in a single company can, among other things, help you avoid the high cost of individual health insurance and other expenses.

There are other ways that information consultants can expand their businesses. If you have your thumb on the pulse of a particular industry, you know the general information and statistics the industry clamors for. All-encompassing industry overviews are valuable tools for the companies that buy them. It's not uncommon for information consultants to produce and sell such overviews.

Hiring Employees

The vast majority of information consultants work independently and subcontract work that they either don't have the skills for or don't have the time for. When information consultants take on employees, they usually don't hire them for the research aspect of the work, but for the administrative aspect. Some consultants have a part-time employee who comes in to take care of paperwork, billing, and other office tasks.

If you decide to hire an employee to help with gathering information, keep in mind that you will have to spend time getting enough work to support both of you. Also, remember that if you hire someone who has the same skills you have, that person is going to expect to make nearly the same amount of money. This is why professionals in this field generally make use of subcontractors instead of taking on employees.

A good job candidate is someone who has potential, but can still learn from you. Teaming up with someone who is at your skill level but has complementary skills could be a benefit, but should only be considered if you can generate at least twice as much work.

For helpful hints about hiring employees, see Chapter 6, "Employees, Benefits, and Policies," in *Start-Up Basics*.

Location, Location, Location

That may be the mantra of the real-estate business, but it's not necessarily the siren song of the information consultant. Because information consulting can be done from home, this section focuses on starting your business as a homebased operation. If your operation ever gets big enough, you can always choose to move to a commercial office later.

The Homebased Business

If you're starting your life as an information consultant from your home, you may have concerns about whether there is enough business in your area to support you in your new career. What if you live in Cowpoke, Indiana, where there's a population of 750, and three other people in the area are already active and experienced information consultants? Well, first off, with a population that small, the other information con-

---

Homebased Help

The decision to expand your business and hire employees doesn't necessarily mean you need to start scouting out office space. The beauty of this age of e-mail and other electronic means of keeping in touch is that you can hire people who work at home. In fact, they don't even really need to be in the same town you're in. With the advent of high-speed Internet access, you can have near-instantaneous conferences with employees who live on the other side of the world. As long as the lines of communication are open, and you've hired people you trust to get the work done (and keep track of their own hours), why not let all your employees work from the comfort of their own home offices?

sultants in your area probably aren't working exclusively for local companies. The fact is, the computer revolution has changed the business world considerably. It's entirely possible for you to do business with clients for years without meeting them in person. Files and messages can be exchanged via e-mail, phone conferences can be held with five different people in five different states participating simultaneously—and no one needs to know you're getting all that communicating done in your pajamas.

One information consultant we spoke to moved herself and her business from California to Texas to take advantage of a lower cost of living. Your rates will be the same whether you live in Alaska or New York, so living in a less

> **! Beware!**
> Your neighbors will probably be happy to know there's someone on the block who works at home and can keep an eye on things. Accepting the occasional package for a neighbor is OK, but don't let your home become the delivery point for the entire neighborhood. Also, be firm with neighbors who think you can take time off during the day and call or drop by too frequently "just to chat."

expensive town can lower the cost of running your business—especially if you work at home. Locating your business in an area with a lower cost of living can be a great advantage, but let's not forget about quality of living. Amelia K., an information consultant and mentor in Sebastopol, California, got into the profession so that she could continue living in the country instead of chasing down jobs in the big city. "I was working in a public library and had been working as a librarian for 12 years," she says. "I was looking for a different career, and I didn't have a lot of options because I live in a rural area and didn't want to move. When I learned about information consulting, I realized that you could do it as a homebased business. I could stay in rural wine country. There's a lot of power in electronic information."

Exceptions to the Rule

Even if your home office isn't located near the businesses you serve, some clients will insist on meeting you in person. There's just no getting around it. This situation seems to be the exception. But, when it happens, you might not get the job without meeting the client face to face. If the client is in your general area, this is not a problem. If the client is in an area that would require you to fly or incur other travel expenses to meet with him or her, you have four options:

1. Incur the expenses yourself and write them off as tax deductions.
2. Tell the client you will need to charge for travel expenses.
3. Convince the client that you can do the job more effectively and start sooner without taking the time to travel.
4. Refer or subcontract the job to an information consultant in the client's area.

▲

Dollar Stretcher

Working from home offers tax advantages that may offset the "self-employment tax" you'll have to pay each year. You can deduct the cost of the square footage of your workspace, as long as that space is used only for work. For more information about the tax advantages of operating a homebased business, see Chapter 17, "Taxes," in *Start-Up Basics*.

Unless it's a really high-paying job for which the traveling will cost you 10 percent or less of what you'll be billing, try to avoid the first choice. Exceptions can be made if you really think the client will become a regular one, and you won't have to make the trip more than once (or at least not for every job). The second choice is really a gamble. Your prospective client may be impressed that you're confident enough to make the demand, may decide that everything can be accomplished over the phone and via e-mail, or may tell you to forget it. The same goes for the third option. The fourth option is a good idea if it looks like you won't be able to work anything out with the client—and an especially good one if you belong to a professional organization. Word will get around that you gave someone a referral, and someone might return the favor.

Face to Face

If you happen to live in a location that's close to those you do business with, take advantage of it. Making the effort to meet with your clients in person shows them that you are serious enough about the job to take time out of your schedule. Talking to clients in person gives you an opportunity to see their reactions as you hash out the details of the projects you'll be undertaking. As anyone who has experience with e-mail can tell you, it can sometimes be difficult to judge emotional reactions without seeing the person you're talking to. Be presentable, polite, professional, and prepared. Spend an hour or two before your meeting familiarizing yourself with the company you'll be providing services to. Most companies have Web sites that provide a brief history of their operation, number of employees, and other information. If the client has given you a brief synopsis of what he or she wants to learn, spend an hour on the Web trying to get an overall picture of the industry, including new developments and trends, to help you speak the same business language as your client.

Breaking the Law?

According to IDC/LINK, an independent market research firm in Framingham, Massachusetts, more than 34 million U.S. households have home offices. Of these, 14.3 million are used by people who are self-employed. Despite these statistics, it is illegal in most areas to run a business out of your home. The laws were originally put into place to keep people from running "sweatshops" in which they had illegally employed

Dollar Stretcher

Keep in mind that you will often have to meet with a client in person only once. If you live within a few hours driving or flying time from a metropolitan area where you will need to meet clients, figure out the cost of flying or driving to the big city around six times a year, and balance that against the amount of money you'll save by living in the suburbs or the country.

people working in their basements. For the most part, these laws are still in place and vary from state to state and even from one neighborhood to another.

Depending on the laws in your area, running your information consulting business out of your home may be illegal. You won't have trucks arriving at your door to deliver goods at all hours of the morning, so your neighbors probably won't care (or even know) what you do for a living. In fact, most people who are self-employed will tell you that their neighbors are happy to have someone in the neighborhood who is at home during the day, whether it's to observe what's going on—possible break-ins, for example—or to have someone their kids can call on in case of an emergency. If you know your neighbors, and you are quietly doing business as an information consultant, you're probably not in danger of being reported. However, if you are operating your business in an apartment or a house that you rent, it's possible that your landlord might not approve. Your best bet is to check the zoning regulations in your neighborhood and take the steps necessary to make sure you're in compliance.

Your Workspace

Selecting an appropriate workspace in your home is important. If possible, use a separate room with a door that closes to isolate you from what's going on in the rest of the house. A garage, basement, or attic usually makes a good home office.

If you have a family or roommates, one of the more difficult aspects of working at home will be getting the people you live with to understand that even though you're at home, you are working. It's kind of a double-edged sword. You may have chosen to work at home to be more available to your family, but that very availability can keep you from getting your work done. Constant interruptions can clearly hurt your business. One simple solution is to provide guidelines for

Bright Idea

If you have a family or housemates, it may be difficult for them to know when you're working. Sometimes you'll be reading. Other times, you'll be pacing the floor thinking about the best way to perform a search. Try putting a sign on the door that says something like "The Doctor Is In," or wearing a "work hat" that lets your housemates know you can't be disturbed.

your housemates about when it is appropriate to interrupt you and when it isn't. This can be a challenge if you have young children around the house, so bear this in mind when you're deciding whether or not to base your office at home.

If you think balancing family life with a homebased business will be too difficult, consider the possibility of renting space for your office outside your home. It may well be that an outside office is not beyond your reach.

Naming Your Business

We've talked about structuring your business and selecting a location for your office. But there's another important early decision you need to make that we've yet to discuss: choosing a name for your business. You'll want to be sure the name you choose conveys what you do. If your name is Jane Doe, you might pick something like Doe Information Services, for example. If you do research in a particular field, you might want to include your expertise in your company's name and go with something like Doe Legal Research. Just make sure you don't limit yourself with your name. Your main business may be legal research, but if you also do competitive analysis for high-tech companies, those potential clients may see your company's name and decide you're not the right person for the job.

Keep in mind that you will probably want the option of creating a Web site with an address that's the same as (or similar to) the name of your business for marketing purposes. Your Web site should be easy to find, and its address, or URL (uniform resource locator), should be easy to remember. For example, if your company is called Doe Information Services, you may want your URL to be www.doeinformation.com.

When you pick a name for your company, make sure that no one is already using the name you want for your business as the domain name for their Web site. Once you come up with a company name that's also available as a domain name for your Web site, you don't need to actually develop a Web site to keep the name. You can make sure it will still be available when you want it by taking ownership of the name. Two popular places to register a domain name are www.networksolutions.com and www.register.com. These Web sites give you all the rules for choosing a Web address, and they also let you know if you've picked a URL that is already owned by someone else. Keeping a domain name registered costs around $35 a year ($25 a year for three years; $30 a year for two years)—a small price to pay to make sure no one creates a Web site with your company's name before you launch your site.

Gadgets
and Gizmos

There are many things to consider when you go into business as an information consultant, but the biggest challenge most people face is making sense of the dizzying array of high-tech devices that are available to make your job easier. In this chapter, we'll take you on a guided tour of the various electronic devices you may need to purchase, including computers, modems, printers, fax machines, and pagers. Some of the devices we'll discuss are absolutely indispensable, while others are merely options to consider before you set up shop.

The Computer: Tool of Your Trade

The most important piece of hardware for an information consultant is the computer. You'll use it to collect information, communicate with clients, and maybe even do some online marketing. Choosing the right computer is especially important because it's likely to be the biggest start-up investment you'll make (aside from your own sweat). There are a number of different types of computers on the market, ranging from bare-bones systems priced under $1,000 to the $40,000-plus systems that graphic artists use for movie special effects and animation. Most information consultants use desktop PCs running some variation of Windows.

We've chosen not to recommend the Macintosh as an option for information consultants for a few reasons. The first is compatibility. While most major software programs are available for both the PC and the Mac, this isn't true for all software. Even Macintosh purists will tell you about the compatibility problems they've had. Incompatibility means that either you'll have trouble opening files from your clients, or—worse—they'll have trouble opening files they receive from you. It also means that the software your clients use may not be available for your computer, which means you won't be able to deliver files in the format they request.

Your job as an information consultant is not to prove a point about your hardware preference, but to communicate with your clients as completely as possible. Right now, that means you should be working on a PC equipped with Windows. This is not to say that Microsoft's offerings are any better than Apple's, just that more people use Windows-based PCs.

If you have a Macintosh and are happy with it, you have probably already worked out solutions to compatibility problems. You'd probably also rather fight than switch. However, Macintoshes won't be covered in this chapter because they are not the industry standard for information consulting. It should be noted that, with the exception of the processor, most of the internal and peripheral devices that are part of a computer system are the same regardless of the operating system. So this chapter should be helpful to Macintosh users as well.

> **Dollar Stretcher**
>
> Many PC manufacturers offer "refurbished machines," computers that have been bought and then returned because they don't work properly. Because most computers are boxes full of components, the companies just replace the parts that don't work and then resell the computers for up to 50 percent off. Refurbished computers can be a great bargain, and they aren't as risky a purchase as they might sound because the warranty is generally the same as that of a new unit.

The Hard Drive: Choosing the Right-Size Toolbox

Your computer's hard drive is the toolbox in which you'll keep the tools of your trade. If you have to choose between size and speed, go with size. At least a 40GB hard drive is a good size and will give you plenty of room for your programs and files, along with the safety margin of extra space that you'll need as upgrades and new programs get bigger.

RAM: Speed on the Fly

RAM is another major contributor to your computer's speed. A good place for information consultants to start is 128 to 256MB RAM, which will allow your programs to run at peak performance and prepare you for new software and upgrades that can hog precious memory. (The high end is better for running Microsoft Windows XP.) Keep an eye on the price of RAM in the ads from computer resellers that appear in your Sunday newspaper. RAM prices tend to rise and fall according to consumer demand. Like the price of gasoline, the price of RAM can also fluctuate because of political and economic conditions in the countries where the chips are produced.

The Eyes Have It

You'll be spending a lot of time working at your computer. That means spending a lot of time looking at a monitor that's little more than a foot from your face. Your parents probably told you that spending too much time in front of the TV was bad for you. To a certain extent, that's also true of spending hours in front of a monitor. Depending on how tolerant you are of such things, your monitor can really bother your eyes and may even give you headaches. Buying a high-quality monitor can help you avoid discomfort.

The first thing to consider in picking a monitor is its size. In short, bigger is generally better. The reason? You'll probably be running more than one software program at a time. Running multiple programs means you'll probably have more than one window open while you work on your computer. The more screen real estate you have, the more things you have simultaneous access to on your computer. Try a 19-inch monitor to give yourself a bit more room to move around. The average price of a 19-inch monitor is around $230.

> **Fun Fact**
>
> The first affordable PCs sold for business use in the late 1970s cost about the same amount as the high-end PCs sold today: around $3,000, including monitor and modem. Of course, the cost of living has nearly doubled since 1980, bringing that early business computer's price to about $6,700 in today's money.

CD-ROM Drives: Is Faster Better?

Another part of your computer system that should be included as a standard component is a CD-ROM drive. Aside from playing your favorite music CDs, you'll be using your CD-ROM drive primarily to install software. Most such drives now have a speed of about 52X, which is fine for your purposes. Many drives are also CD-RW (CD rewriteable) and DVD combination drives, which allow you to access many more types of applications.

Should You Get a Laptop?

Today's portable, or laptop, computers are lighter and faster than ever, but their compact size and speed come at a premium price. However, if you travel a lot, like to work outside of your office (perhaps on your deck or at the local coffee shop?), or make computer-based presentations, you should consider a laptop. You can always use it in your office more comfortably with the aid of a port replicator or docking station, connectors with names right out of "Star Trek" that allow you to plug in a full-sized keyboard and monitor.

With your laptop, be sure to have an Ethernet LAN (local-area network) or wireless networking circuit card on hand to allow you to tap into the Internet wherever you can find access. An increasing number of hotels and other business facilities (even coffee shops) provide this link. Test these connections before you travel, so you don't run into difficulty on the road.

Choosing a laptop is a more personal and ergonomics-minded decision than choosing a conventional system, with more variables to consider—such as the applications you will run, battery life required, graphics requirements, weight, and more. Consider what you can reasonably carry, given that you will also be lugging one or two batteries, a protective carrying case, and more. You may also consider renting before you buy to gauge your comfort with various screen types and keyboard sizes; specifications change almost daily.

As a rule of thumb, laptops cost twice as much as desktop systems for about half the computer. Most basic machines have a 14- to 15-inch display, 256MB RAM, a 1.3+ GHz

Dollar Stretcher

If you frequently have to send large files to clients, consider getting a CD-R drive. A CD-R drive lets you copy information onto a CD that can be read from your client's CD-ROM drive. A CD-R drive holds 650MB of data, not quite as much as a Zip drive's 750MB, but more systems have CD-ROM than Zip drives. The compact discs cost about $1 to $3 each, as opposed to $10 to $15 each for Zip disks. The CD-R drive itself costs $100 to $120, compared with the Zip drive's price of about $180. The downside is, you have to spend some time mastering the process of copying data onto the disk.

processor, a 30GB hard drive, integrated video and sound, and an Ethernet card with slots for PC cards for wireless connections. These systems go for as little as $800 to $900, but you get what you pay for.

One fast-growing new technology is called "Centrino," for built-in wireless networking. Going wireless has obvious benefits, but it opens major security issues, and you will need to consider data encryption, personalized network IDs, and more.

Talking to the Digital World

Dial-up modems transmit information at 56K per second. Although a few years ago, 56K modems were state-of-the-art, they are now found by Internet-dependent professionals to be slow and inconvenient. Thankfully, demonstrably faster Internet connections have become available in most parts of the country for more money. We'll run through them to give you an idea of what's available if you find that the amount of time you wait for Web pages to display—or to download software or multimedia files—slows you down:

- *Dual 56K modem.* Capable of 112K, a dual 56K modem is a good, reasonably priced alternative for those who need higher-speed Internet connections. It costs about $150 for setup plus an additional $10 charge from your ISP for multiple-line access (only a few ISPs support multiple-line connections, so you'll have to do some checking and maybe even switch ISPs to use this option).

- *Cable modem.* Cable modems are the fastest Internet-access technology available to home PC users. As the name implies, cable modems are offered by the same companies that provide cable TV service. Where available, cable modems are inexpensive and really fast, achieving speeds of up to 38MB/second (although they rarely reach this limit). Installation costs $25 to $100, depending on whether you do it yourself; the modem costs about $50 to $100 to purchase but can also be leased for a few dollars each month. The service charge for access is about $40 to $50 per month; discounts are often available.

- *DSL line and modem.* DSL, which sends data over telephone lines, offers tremendous speed increases over ISDN. It allows connection speeds of up to 7.1 Mbps—scores of times faster than 56K access and ISDN—and even

Dollar Stretcher

Everyone—especially information consultants—can use faster Internet access. The two competing technologies right now are cable modems and DSL. Although the cable companies have about a two-to-one lead in customers right now, phone companies are competing fiercely to narrow the gap. As a result, both phone and cable providers often offer rebates, discounts, and other price breaks. So do a little comparison shopping.

faster access speeds are becoming available. DSL installation costs $35 to $100, depending on whether you install the device yourself. A DSL modem costs $200, and basic DSL service from your local phone company costs from $40 to $80 per month where it's available, depending on the speed you choose. The benefit is that DSL is a dedicated line, which means it's always connected to the Internet—your computer doesn't need to dial out for access.

- *ISDN line.* The other step up in speed and price is the ISDN connection. Most ISDN connections give you two 64Kbps lines so you can use one line as your voice or fax line and the other for data, or you can use both lines for data to give you connection speeds of up to 128Kbps or higher (with digital technology). To use it, your local phone company must install an ISDN line, and you must purchase an ISDN modem as well as pay a monthly fee for using the line. ISDN can be hard to find, and its costs hard to research; the service is not widely available, especially in areas that have cable modems or DSL.

Backup Devices and Firewalls: Better Safe than Sorry

The conventional wisdom of some experts in the computer industry is that there are only two kinds of computer users: those who have had a hard-drive crash and those who will. The fact is, hard-drive crashes are a lot rarer now than they were a few years ago due to improvements in design. However, as an information consultant, you're not just playing around with your computer—it's central to your business. The information you collect and the documents you work on need protection against equipment failure and other unforeseeable events such as fire or theft.

At the end of each working day, you need to copy your files onto some type of storage device so that in the event of a catastrophe you can copy your working files onto another computer and get back to work without having to start the whole project over again. Some people even remove their backup tapes or disks and put them in a safe (possibly fireproof) place so that if their computers get stolen or their offices burn down, at least they can continue to work.

Here's a story that illustrates the importance of backing up data, and shows how unpredictable life can be. One information consultant we talked to was working late at night on his notebook computer, in which he had invested a lot of money. When he finished

Smart Tip

Another option for backing up your system is to copy your files to an Internet server. While security issues have been debated, the companies that offer this service almost always guarantee the security of your files. Many big corporations back up their data to computers at remote locations called "hot sites," so they can recover their information in case of a natural disaster. These are both backup options you might want to explore.

working, he left the notebook computer open on his desk. The family cat came along and—for lack of a nicer way to put it—threw up on the computer's keyboard. Well, the keyboard on a notebook computer is right on top of the system's internals. So when our consultant woke up, he not only had a mess on his hands but a computer that no longer worked. The bad part was that this type of "natural disaster" was not covered in the computer's warranty, so he had to buy a new computer. But even worse, he had a few thousand dollars' worth of work on the computer that could not be recovered. It cost him a sizable amount of money because, even though his clients extended their deadlines after hearing his funny story, he had to spend weeks recompiling all the lost data—weeks he could have spent working on other projects.

Bargain Shopping

You can practice your research skills by trying to find the best deals on computer hardware online. The Internet has a number of sites that post product reviews and other sites that offer goods for sale. Be wary of sites that offer both. These sites may tend to give positive reviews about the products they have for sale.

Whether your Internet purchase will include sales tax is a state-by-state proposition. As of this writing, 45 states and the District of Columbia charge sales tax for Internet sales. If you're spending a few thousand dollars, you may want to consider the location of your online retailer. Taxes aside, products sold over the Internet are often cheaper than those sold in conventional brick-and-mortar shops, because online retailers don't have to lease store space or pay a bunch of employees. However, this can sometimes result in poor customer service if you have a problem.

Find out as much as you can about your peers' experiences with buying computer products over the Internet, and pick a company you think will give you the service you need.

Companies that sell computer products online include:

○ *PC Connection:* www.pcconnection.com
○ *PC Zone:* www.pczone.com
○ *CompUSA:* www.compusa.com
○ *Gateway Computer:* www.gateway.com
○ *Dell Computer:* www.dell.com

Web sites that offer computer-product reviews include:

○ *CNET:* www.cnet.com
○ *PC World:* www.pcworld.com
○ *Computer Shopper:* www.computershopper.com
○ *CNET Shopper.com:* www.cnet.com

That said, you need to make sure you have a backup device for your computer. It's also a good idea to archive the data files from all your previous projects in a location that's not on your hard drive so you can refer to them for information without filling up your hard drive with files you aren't working on. Let's look at your options. First off, while nearly all PCs include a floppy-disk drive, at 1.44MB floppy disks just don't have the capacity to support a daily backup of every project you're working on. That leaves us with two other options:

1. *High-capacity removable disk drives:* There are many disk-based data storage options available, but the most popular is Iomega's Zip drive. The Zip drive holds up to 750MB of data, so it works well to back up and archive your data. Its new format is easier to use than before; it acts like a big floppy disk. It has also become so popular that it comes as standard equipment on many computers. The drive itself costs around $180, and the disks are priced at about $10 to $15 each (you can spend $40 for a three-pack). Because of the Zip drive's popularity, most of your clients will have one, so you can use the disks to deliver data to them. The downside to the Zip is that it can't hold enough data to back up your entire hard drive.

    The CD-RW drive is another data storage option, one that has come into vogue as its price has dropped. A typical CD-RW drive costs about $100 to $120. The discs, which look like CD-ROMs, cost pennies; you can get a 100-disc spindle for about $30 (rebates often lower the price to about $15). They hold 650MB of data. The benefit of CD-RW discs is they can be erased and recorded over multiple times. You can deliver data to your clients on the discs because they can be read by most CD-ROM drives (some older CD-ROM drives, however, may not be able to read discs created using a CD-RW drive). The downside to CD-RW drives is that, like Zip drives, they aren't big enough to hold all the contents of your hard drive. In addition, even when formatted for Direct-CD packet writing (wherein you "write" to them as if they were a floppy disk), they are a little tricky for many to use effectively as a backup. If you can master the CD writing and making of backups, this may work well because every computer system has a CD drive.

2. *High-capacity removable tape drive:* If you're looking to back up more than just your data files, you'll most likely need to purchase a tape drive. Tape drives are available in sizes that will back up everything from a single hard drive to an entire network. For our purposes, a drive that will back up 20 to 40GB is about the right size. These tape drives cost upwards of $200, with tapes selling for about $35 to $45 each.

    If you back up to a tape drive and keep the tape in a safe place, you can restore the entire contents of your computer. This capability can save you a lot of time in recovering from an emergency. If you experience a hard-drive crash, just install a new hard drive, and the tape backup will put everything you had on the old drive onto the new drive. The downside to these devices is that, compared with CD-RW and Zip drives, they can be slow and cumbersome; they are also less reliable. They also can't be used to distribute files to clients, but then, that's really not their purpose. They're intended to allow you to recover from a disaster and get your business up and running as quickly and painlessly as possible.

Also in the area of "Secure your data!" is the firewall, a hardware or software barrier that keeps intruders from gaining access through your Internet connection to information on your computer. You—just like government agencies or credit card companies—can fall victim to hackers. Hacking is more possible with high-speed connections, so if you have high-speed or wireless Internet access, you should use some kind of firewall.

Computer experts tend to prefer hardware firewalls, which physically barricade others from tapping into your system. For a small, homebased business, something straight off the shelf with only minor customizations for password and so on can be fine. These simple, $50 to $150 devices are available at retailers such as CompUSA and Best Buy.

Computer experts don't recommend software firewalls because they add unnecessary layers to system resources. Users also tend to answer prompts incorrectly, locking themselves out of their own systems. Software solutions are also more prone to hack attempts and "cracks" that defeat the security offered.

Beware!

While many printers claim to produce photo-quality printouts, this claim is often based on the use of special paper that can cost up to a dollar per sheet. When you're shopping for a printer, look for one that performs the tasks you need for the lowest price and with the best print quality. Take a few sheets of reasonably priced paper with you, and ask to see demonstrations on it. As an information consultant, you want professional-looking printouts and a low cost per page.

Printers: Getting It on Paper

As an information consultant, you'll be finding and downloading a lot of information. Many people in the business will tell you they've tried doing all their reading on-screen to save printing costs but have found that printing things out lets them be more mobile and flexible in their work habits. When you print out information, you can read it while you're eating lunch or sitting in the park.

Let's assume that you'll be printing out a lot of stuff. That means you should look at the cost per page of any printer you buy. From a cost-per-page standpoint, laser printers beat inkjets by a wide margin. But that won't help you if you need to print in color, because (the affordable) laser printers will only give you black-and-white.

Generally, when you're first starting out, it's a good idea to go with an inkjet printer that will allow you to print in black-and-white most of the time and swap in a color cartridge only when you need it. After a year or so, you'll know whether you should invest in a laser printer for lower overall cost and cleaner printouts. If you buy a laser printer later, you can use your old inkjet for color when you need it.

If you're pretty sure you won't be producing reports for clients (maybe you already know someone who can do this for you, or you plan to avoid it entirely by finding someone with these skills), you may not need to print anything other than black text in your daily work. If that's the case, spending the extra couple hundred dollars for a laser printer is a worthwhile investment. Even if you occasionally have to print reports in color, most full-service copy centers will do the job for you for a low price (which you may even be able to charge to your client, depending on your contract).

Facts by Fax

A fax machine is an absolute necessity for shooting off printed documents and for receiving responses from those you've requested information from. And yes, you really need a separate fax machine. We're not behind the times; we know computers are capable of sending and receiving faxes. But being able to fax from your computer is only convenient if what you're sending is an electronic file that's already in your computer. In that case, you're using the receiving fax machine as a printer, and the result will be a really clean-looking fax. If you need to send a photocopied magazine page to your client, however, you're out of luck unless you have a scanner (more on that on page 43). Try as you might, you just can't stuff a piece of paper into your computer and have it print out on the other end of the phone line.

As far as receiving faxes is concerned, clients will tire quickly of having to call to let you know when they're sending faxes so that you can start the fax software on your computer. Are your clients and the agencies you'll need to contact for information all located in the same time zone as you? If not, receiving faxes on your computer will mean leaving your computer on 24 hours a day.

For little more than $100 and the cost of a phone line, you can receive faxes around the clock and send them without interrupting the work you're doing on your computer. It's a worthwhile investment even if your only goal is to put the wear and tear on the cheaper—much cheaper—device. When you're shopping for a fax machine, read reviews, compare prices, check warranties, and make sure you know the price of consumables.

> **Smart Tip** Tip...
> Avoid the old-fashioned "thermal" fax machines. They require special paper, and the print quality is not very good. If you opt for a plain-paper fax machine, you can usually use the same paper you use in your printer, giving you one less consumable to keep track of.

Do You Copy?

Copier prices have come down for units with limited functions; they start at around $200. Of course, if you need two copies of a document, you can always use your printer to make them. Information consultants find that for larger jobs, it's just as easy to use the local copy shop, so it's probably not worth it to buy a dedicated copier. As for multifunction devices, the cost of making your copies at the local copy shop is about the same as the cost of making them on a multifunction device for small numbers of copies, but significantly less for making large numbers of copies. Using a copy shop also spares your multifunction device unnecessary wear and tear. Think of your all-in-one office machine as a convenience for making a few copies once in a while, and take the big jobs, such as mass mailings and large reports, to your local copy shop.

Scanners, Anyone?

As an information consultant, you'll really have little use for a scanner. It can come in handy if you want to put a photograph in a presentation, but aside from that, you probably won't need one. If you find that you need a scanner for integrating pictures into presentations, you can pick one up for anywhere between $50 and $200 (depending on how many lines it scans and how many functions it offers), with the average slightly less than $100.

Staying in Touch: Phone Lines

Now it's time to decide what you need from your local telephone-service provider. To provide optimum service for your clients, you really should have three phone lines: one for Internet access (if you still have dial-up service), one for voice calls, and one for your fax machine. Many consultants get by with two phone lines. The trick is to use one of the lines for two purposes. Maybe you'll receive only a couple of faxes a month. In that case, you can have one phone line do double duty as your Internet access line and your fax line by using a little plug called a phone jack splitter, which allows you to connect your computer and your fax machine to the same phone line. (You can buy a splitter from your local Radio Shack for around $6.) The problem is that when you're expecting a fax, you'll have to avoid using the Internet to leave the line available to

> **Bright Idea**
>
> Many modems give you the option of having the call-waiting beep disconnect the modem connection. If you use the same phone line for your fax machine and modem, for example, you can let the beep disconnect your Internet access to allow a fax to come in. This option can be turned on and off, in case you're downloading something and don't want the line disconnected.

▲

receive it. You could also combine your phone and fax to leave your online access available, or combine your voice line and online access to leave your fax machine available, depending on your needs.

In any case, while it's possible to operate with just two phone lines, your best bet is to have three. The exception is if you install a DSL (or, more rarely, an ISDN) line, which, through some miracle of science and telephony, allows you to use one line to simultaneously access online services and conduct phone calls or send faxes. A cable modem will also eliminate the need for a third phone line.

Paging Dr. Info...

Does an information consultant need a pager and/or a cell phone? From a business perspective, cell phones are convenient, especially if you travel a lot. The problem is that most information consultants turn them off to keep from running down the battery or because they're busy gathering information. The decision about whether to have a cell phone is going to be a personal

Bright Idea

If you use a pager, check out the nifty options the pager service provider offers. Many pager services notify you with a page whenever a call comes in on your office phone. Others let people page you instead of leaving a message if you don't answer the phone.

More Fun Toys

In addition to the standard equipment you need to start your information consulting business, there are some optional and inexpensive services that you may choose to include in your office. For example, it's now possible to send and receive faxes via e-mail using services such as j2.com (formerly JFAX.COM, found at either www.j2.com or www.jfax.com), which can be handy if you travel a lot and need to get your faxes while you're away from the office.

Other useful services can be purchased from your local phone company. Caller ID shows you the name and phone number of the person who's calling so you can pick up important calls (or avoid picking up personal calls when you're busy). Caller ID is also available for your call-waiting service so you can see who's calling, just in case you take a personal call while you're waiting for an important one.

You can also receive e-mail on your cell phone or pager, have your office phone forward calls to your cell phone, or receive a page when someone leaves you a voice-mail message. Keep an eye out for other services that may help your business run more smoothly.

one based on the type of consulting you do. One thing cell phones are especially good for, however, is checking your voice-mail messages. Believe it or not, they're also good for making yourself less available and giving yourself a little more freedom to enjoy being self-employed. Clients don't always call back when they say they will. Saying you have an appointment but will answer their calls on your cell phone not only gives them the impression that you are in high demand but also that you'll interrupt your other meeting to take care of their more pressing business. There's no need to tell them you're going to be sitting in the park or going for a walk rather than sitting in the house waiting for their calls.

Pagers are especially good for lowering your cell phone bill. Pager service costs only around $10 to $15 a month plus the one-time charge ($40 to $100) of buying the pager. If you have a pager, you don't even have to tell your clients you have a cell phone. Just use the cell phone to return your pages if you're away from a cheaper means of contacting them. If you combine the two little gadgets, you can appear to be constantly available for around $30 a month, while giving yourself the opportunity to leave the office without guilt.

Protecting Your Investments: Extended Warranties and Insurance

For equipment that could shut down your business if it breaks down, try to buy from a store that offers extended warranties and loaner units. That way, if you experience a breakdown, you'll get a comparable device—be it a computer, a printer, or fax machine—to use while your broken equipment is in the shop. Keep in mind that a loaner computer isn't going to help you much if you haven't backed up your work.

How long a warranty should you get? Many high-tech equipment resellers, such as Circuit City, Office Depot, and CompUSA, offer extended warranties that can add up to three years to equipment manufacturers' standard one-year plans. The price of each extra year is based on the equipment purchase price. However, you probably don't need to have more than a two-year (total) warranty. Two years is a long time in the world of high-tech equipment, and you'll most likely be looking to upgrade to the latest and greatest new gadgets after that time has elapsed. You'll probably be able to replace the printer you buy with a newer unit that's cheaper to run and just plain more advanced well before those two years are up.

Dollar Stretcher
Some computer retailers offer a three-year warranty at no charge, while others charge you a substantial amount to extend the warranty. Keep this in mind when looking at the price tag. A slightly more expensive computer with a longer warranty may have a lower total cost.

Whatever the length of the warranty, try to get one that will replace the faulty equipment if it's in the shop for a certain amount of time. Usually, these extended warranties will replace your equipment with an "equivalent unit." If your aging printer or other device is no longer available, you may just get a brand-new, more modern unit if your old one goes to that computer superstore in the sky.

For more tips on buying office equipment, check out Chapter 8, "Computers," in *Start-Up Basics*.

The Information Consultant's Office Checklist

Use this sample checklist to add up your expenditures on office equipment.

Items	Prices
❑ Current software and computer with a 40GB hard drive, 256MB RAM, and CD-RW drive, plus a network card for high-speed Internet connections	$_____
❑ 19-inch monitor	_____
❑ Zip drive (optional)	_____
❑ Zip disks (only if you opt for the drive)	_____
❑ Tape drive	_____
❑ Tape cartridges	_____
❑ CD-RW drive	_____
❑ CD-RW discs	_____
❑ Laser or inkjet printer	_____
❑ Toner or inkjet cartridges	_____
❑ Fax machine	_____
❑ Scanner	_____
❑ Phone lines (one or two lines with voice mail)	_____
❑ Internet Access Provider	_____
❑ Cable modem or DSL installation	_____
❑ Pager	_____
❑ Cell phone	_____
Total Office Equipment Expenditures	$_____

Searching for
Software

Having high-tech gadgets and gizmos at your disposal may be the most liberating thing the computer age has to offer in terms of increased productivity. In the case of computer hardware, you have many options to choose from based on your needs and finances. Your most important hardware need is to be able to run the appropriate software for your business. Software programs are the tools that let you write letters, develop e-mail correspondence, find information on the Internet, and much more.

Browse through a catalog from a company that sells computer software, and you're faced with a dizzying number of software options—all of which claim they will help your business run more efficiently. When you're choosing software, you are once again faced with the uncomfortable task of finding a balance between what you need and what you can afford. Inevitably, just as with hardware, you'll become aware of new needs as your business develops and will have to adapt your arsenal of tools periodically to meet those needs.

The Basics: Web Access, E-Mail, and Word Processing

The three most important tools you'll use as an information consultant are the Internet, e-mail, and word processing software. Yes, you'll use other software, but the ability to gather information and contact people via the Internet, as well as create written materials such as letters, reports, and (most important) invoices is invaluable. Internet access and e-mail are closely related, because you'll be dialing in to the same ISP for both and possibly even accessing your e-mail from the ISP's Web site. So let's take a look at these Web-related software programs first.

Choosing an ISP

Your ISP is the front door to the world of electronic communications, whether you are sending e-mail or browsing the Internet for information. Both of these activities are handled by the same type of computer, called a server, over the same transmission lines. You use your computer's modem to connect to your ISP's server, which is a powerful computer that is connected to other servers around the world that are all linked together. The reason you don't have to pay long-distance charges when you send e-mail or access a Web page in another part of the world is that these Internet servers each contact the nearest server within local phone calling distance. It's a web of

Bright Idea

CompuServe, now owned by AOL, built its reputation by providing numerous online forums or discussion groups in which people with similar interests share ideas. Some information consultants sign up for CompuServe as a second ISP at an hourly rate just to get access to these forums, some of which are hosted by hardware and software vendors you can send messages to directly if you have problems with a computer product. Other Internet forum possibilities include topical e-mail lists to which you can subscribe, possibly through www.topica.com, and news group discussions you can browse.

local phone calls made by computers, which may explain why telephone companies are now getting into the ISP business. Because the phone companies can't recoup the long-distance charges they're missing out on, many are offering their own Internet access services.

In prior years, users had to choose between low-cost, no-frills, often hard to set up Internet service and slicker, prepackaged, higher-cost services such as America Online (AOL) and Microsoft Network (MSN), which also include exclusive "brand" content. Those distinctions have largely blurred, as lower-cost ISPs (such as EarthLink and MindSpring) now offer easily installed software, bright graphical interfaces, and more "bells and whistles" for using the Internet.

> **Beware!**
> Before choosing an ISP, talk to as many people as you can to find out whether they like the service and find it easy to connect at all times. Make sure the people you talk to are professionals who use their Internet access for business. People who use the Internet for fun simply don't have to go online as often, so they may not notice any connection problems.

Note that when information consultants talk about online services, they are generally referring to dial-in databases or subscription services like Dialog and Lexis-Nexis (just to make things even more confusing).

The big proprietary-content ISPs such as AOL, MSN, and the downscaled CompuServe still offer a variety of extra services, including online forums, but they are mostly geared toward consumers rather than business professionals. The phone companies also provide Internet access, often through a special promotion, adding it to your phone bill. Most ISPs charge $20 to $25 per month.

If you're new to the online world and want to get up and running quickly, take a look at the larger ISPs. They offer customized interfaces that are easier to set up and use than stand-alone e-mail packages and Web browsers. If you decide to switch to using software other than what the ISP provides, you can gradually change over to it without having to worry about downtime while you set it up. The point here is, whether you use the software provided by the ISP or decide to use another type, the procedure for connecting is the same. You really don't have to use the software the ISP provides to access anything other than the special services it offers.

Why would you switch to a smaller local company or one that doesn't provide its own software? First, you may find (with any ISP, not just the big guys) that you have trouble connecting during certain times of the day. Due to their popularity, some ISPs sell more services than they can support (kind of like gym memberships). This means they don't have enough phone lines to allow everyone to connect at the same time. Another reason you might decide to switch is if you don't need the ease of use the big ISPs offer, and you're looking for a company that provides other perks such as extra e-mail addresses, a larger amount of space for your Web site (if you have one), or an area where you can post large files for download (most ISPs limit the size of e-mail attachments— the quickest way to transfer large files without sending them on disk).

Web Browsers

The two most popular Web browsers are Microsoft's Internet Explorer and Netscape's Navigator. While there have been heated debates about which one is better, both are capable of getting you around online. Just about every Web site in the world can be viewed using either of these programs. In fact, even if the software your ISP provides doesn't look a heck of a lot like either of these browsers, it probably is.

Microsoft and Netscape make money off their browsers by licensing them to ISPs and allowing them to customize them. This is the main reason that these programs can be downloaded off the Internet for free. Why would you want to use a downloaded version of either of these programs instead of the customized version your ISP gives you? The customized versions tend to be bigger and slower due to all the bells and whistles they offer. Downloading the programs separately will probably be your first experiment in deciding how you want to access information online. For example, maybe the customized browser provided by your ISP allows you to see if your friends are online, or send and receive e-mail automatically. Functions like these tend to slow down your computer and your Internet access. If you use the stand-alone version of the browser to connect to your ISP, your computer's efforts won't be used for anything but research. Keep your ISP's software installed while you work on setting things up on your own—and don't mess with anything you don't feel comfortable with.

E-Mail Programs

Most of the e-mail programs provided by ISPs or as a part of Navigator or Internet Explorer give you the most basic e-mail functionality. Why would you want anything more than simple and quick access to sending and receiving e-mail? The reason you might want to look into buying a stand-alone e-mail program like Microsoft's Outlook or Lotus Notes' cc:Mail is that these programs offer extended e-mail options. Some make sending e-mail to large lists of people easier, others combine your e-mail program with a contact manager, allowing you to keep all the information about your contacts in one place, and still others let you sort your incoming mail based on who it came from and what the subject is.

⚠ Beware!

If you're planning to send out a newsletter or large numbers of questionnaires via e-mail, check with your ISP to find out whether it limits the number of recipients for a single message. For example, if you send out an e-mail newsletter with 51 recipients, the ISP may assume it's some kind of unsolicited advertisement (also known as spam) and automatically delete the message.

Of course you may not need anything more than basic e-mail for your business, but if you start to find it cumbersome or if you want additional features, shop around and find an e-mail program that does what you need. Once again, setting up these programs will require you to be somewhat adept at configuring your computer.

Word Processors

If your clients aren't using the same word processing program that you are, chances are they won't be able to open the files you give them. Even if they are able to open them, the translation capabilities of different word processing programs vary. Your original formatting (the way the text is placed on the page) may look childish at best once it's translated, because these programs understand text characters better than formatting instructions.

Smart Tip *Tip...*

You may need to have more than one word processing program to produce files that are compatible with what your clients use. Software programs in the same category aren't all that much different from each other, and it's better not to get into discussions with clients about which program is better. Do it their way.

Don't Copy That Floppy!

Why purchase software when you can simply borrow the installation disks from a friend who already has the program? Well, for one thing, it's illegal. While it's unlikely that you as an individual consumer will get caught, software companies have been aggressively seeking out and prosecuting companies with as few as 20 employees and making them pay up.

Aside from the ethical issues, there are a few other problems with trying to get off cheap where software is concerned. First, it brings the price of software up for everyone. Part of the reason software is expensive in the first place is that the manufacturers know a large percentage of people are using their products for free. They make up for the lost revenue by raising prices. Another problem is that if you have trouble with the software or you have questions about how to use it, you can't call for technical support. You also can't reinstall the software without borrowing the disks again. When the time comes to upgrade the software (perhaps because a client upgraded and you need to be compatible), you'll have to purchase the entire application rather than the much less expensive upgrade because you aren't a registered owner. No matter how tempting it is to get software for free, it will cost you money in the long run.

If you know what word processing program your clients use, that's what you need to use to enable them to open the files you send them. Right now, Microsoft Word is the closest thing to a standard in word processing software. It's probably the best program for transferring files between Windows and Macintosh platforms.

Keeping House: Spreadsheets, Databases, and Contact Managers

When you're an information consultant, data is your business. Computer software for handling data can help you store and easily access your information. Spreadsheet, database, and contact management software programs are the electronic filing cabinets for keeping all your information in order. While related and certainly similar, each of these types of applications has different strengths. Let's take a look at what each type of data-organizing software can do for your business.

Spreadsheets: Just the Facts

Spreadsheet programs can be used to organize a multitude of different types of data. The advantage to using spreadsheet programs is that you can sort information, swap the columns around, and even automatically add up numerical data. For example, instead of using a spreadsheet to keep track of company, product, and contact information, you could use it to keep track of your income. To do this, you would replace the "Product" column with a "Project" one where you give a short description of the work you did, and replace the "Price" column with one for "Invoice Amount." You could then tell the program that row four is where you want to see your total income, and the program would automatically do the addition for you, keeping a running total of income as you entered the data and received the checks.

Spreadsheet programs are extremely flexible. You can use them to keep track of just about any kind of data—even bookkeeping. They are cheaper than accounting programs and can be used for many other purposes. You could sort data by product, price, company name, or phone number. You could also combine different sorts so that, for example, the program looks at the price first (putting the rows with the highest or lowest price at the top of the list), then alphabetically. Most word

> ### Fun Fact
> The first electronic spreadsheet program, VisiCalc, was invented in the late 1970s by software pioneer Dan Bricklin. At that time, software products were rarely granted patents. Had he been able to patent his idea, he'd be collecting royalties from every software company that produces spreadsheet programs.

processing programs will also let you import spreadsheets and turn them into charts or graphs. A spreadsheet program like Microsoft Excel is the minimum spreadsheet tool you should have for keeping track of data.

Database Software: Quick and Easy Data

Database programs handle data in an easy-to-access manner, which makes them the next step up from spreadsheet programs. These programs divide sets of data into individual records that can be easily searched and organized. Database programs like Microsoft Access allow you to either import the raw data you have in spreadsheets or set up records with fields in which you can fill in the data.

Each line in the spreadsheet becomes its own individual record and can be organized according to what is in each field (for example, alphabetically by company name). Using the application's search capabilities, you can dig through the database looking for specific information. While databases don't really hold any more information than spreadsheets, they are much easier on the eyes and look a lot more professional to clients. Databases can also be really handy for keeping track of information you've gathered for future reference. Rather than digging through a filing cabinet for information, you can search your database in a few seconds. If you update your database during or after each job, you'll have your own set of reference materials to search through. This can be especially helpful if you frequently take on information consulting jobs in the same field or for the same clients.

Contact Managers: People Data

A contact manager is a type of database program that's set up specifically for organizing and storing data about people. The fields in a contact manager program help you keep track of contact information about your clients and resources, sometimes even offering you fields for minute bits of information such as birthdays, the names of assistants, anniversaries, nicknames, and even the names of your contacts' spouses. Using a contact manager, you can also keep notes about the times and dates that you spoke to clients. It's kind of like a really fancy electronic Rolodex.

Contact management software varies depending on the specific program you buy. Many contact management programs allow you to view your contacts in many different ways. For example, you could find every contact who works at a certain company or search for every contact within a certain area code.

Tip...

Smart Tip
Make sure you have your contacts' information (at least their phone numbers) in some form that you can carry around with you, whether it's in your PDA, a little black book, or a printout from your contact manager program. You may not always be sitting in front of your computer when you need to contact a client.

Some contact managers also double as e-mail programs, allowing you to click on the name of the contact to create a message without typing in the person's e-mail address. Others let you print mailing labels by picking names on a list. This feature can be pretty handy when you want to send out holiday cards or press releases. If you want to take your contact data with you, many contact managers will let you print out your records in a number of forms that can be put into a day planner with just a bit of cutting and hole punching.

Final Analysis:
What You Need, and What It Costs

Since you'll probably get basic e-mail software and a Web browser from your ISP, the two most important software tools you'll purchase will be a word processing program and a spreadsheet program, each of which will set you back about $100 to $200. If you can afford them, a contact manager and a database program can help keep things organized. It's a lot easier to be well-organized from the start than it is to wait for a year and then switch to keeping track of your data electronically. At some point, you'll have to spend a few days or even weeks keying in all of that data or importing it from spreadsheets. Time is money.

If you do decide to start out with the basics, adding a contact manager or database program later will cost more than a spreadsheet or word processing program—around $150 to $300. If you plan to buy all the software programs you need at the same time, your best bet is to go with an office suite package. Microsoft and Lotus both offer comparable suites that include all the software tools you need to keep your business organized, such as a word processor, spreadsheet, presentation manager, and a tool integrating e-mail, calendar, and document management. If you buy one of these suites, you'll save at least 25 percent off the price of buying each of the included products separately. Make sure all your software is compatible not only among the different applications (so you can swap data back and forth) but also with what your clients are using.

Other Software:
Your Hard Drive Is the Limit

In this chapter, we looked at the software packages that are of particular importance to information consultants. Some other applications you may want to consider buying include: financial management programs (which we'll look at in Chapter 9), presentation programs that help you present data in the form of computer-based "slide shows," and Web site development programs. Some of these programs are included in office suites, so you can experiment with them before you actually need them. How high-tech you get with your software is only limited by the depth of your pockets and the space on your hard drive. Check out Chapter 8, "Computers," in *Start-Up Basics* for more ideas about software programs that you may find useful.

Information Consultant Software Checklist

Use this checklist to keep track of your expenditures on software. Optional software is at the bottom of the list.

Items	Prices
❑ E-mail software	$_____
❑ Word processing software	_____
❑ Contact manager	_____
❑ Spreadsheet program	_____
❑ Database program	_____
OR	
❑ Office software suite	_____
❑ ISP software	_____
❑ Web browser	(Free!)
Optional Software	
❑ Web site development software	_____
❑ Presentation software (such as Microsoft PowerPoint)	_____
❑ Financial management software	_____
Total Software Expenditures	$_____

6

Dollars
and Sense

As you probably gathered from Chapters 4 and 5, the amount of money you can spend on hardware and software ranges from next to nothing to a substantial start-up expense. The same is true for office basics like a chair, a desk, and a file cabinet.

There are two ways to go about buying the equipment you need to launch your information consulting business. Your first option is to upgrade your office and equipment as needed. You can get by at first with an inexpensive computer, a few software programs, the least expensive Internet access you can find, and the furniture and office supplies you have around the house. From there, you can slowly work up to a cable modem hookup or DSL line, a super-fast computer, and the chair that looks like it came from the bridge of the Starship *Enterprise*.

> ## Dollar Stretcher
>
> Some computer retailers offer programs in which you can trade in a PC for a more modern one at a greatly reduced price within a few years. If you are only tentatively entering the world of entrepreneurship, see if you can lease a computer with an option to buy.

Your second option is to start out spending a bunch of money and be prepared for just about anything. If you have the money, get the best equipment you can right from the start. Why? Upgrading any part of your business will cause downtime—time when you are not doing work that you're billing for. Even switching to a new desk will probably cost you a day of work while you rearrange your office.

Good Money after Bad

The notion of throwing good money after bad comes into play in a pretty big way when you purchase equipment for your business. If you buy a computer that's too old or too slow to run the programs you need, you'll end up buying a new one much sooner than if you had bitten the bullet and made the initial investment in a higher-quality model. Let's say the cheap computer costs $800 and the hot rod costs $1,500. If you fail to assess your needs properly and have to buy two computers in the same year, you've actually spent $2,300 to end up with the same computer on your desk. The same thing goes for office furniture. If you buy the $100 chair to save money, and then buy the $300 chair the next month because your back is killing you, you haven't assessed your needs correctly.

Seeing into the future isn't that easy, so you may make mistakes in trying to anticipate exactly what equipment you'll need. As your business becomes more successful, reward yourself and your business by getting the best equipment you can afford. Over the course of a few years, it can really save you money.

How Much Will You Spend?

In this section, we'll look at how much you're likely to spend on office equipment. The "Equipment Expenses" chart on page 60 gives you two sets of equipment cost estimates: one for aspiring information consultants who are on a budget and another for those with plenty of start-up capital. The high-end list will include office furniture and the low-end will assume you can get by with the furniture you have now. Both the high- and the low-end estimates will assume you'll be working at home (like most information consultants) and starting as a one-person operation. Neither will assume that you need software to build a Web site, because that will be a decision you make when you figure out how to market your services (see Chapter 8). The low-end estimate also assumes that you'll be using software provided by your ISP for both Internet access and e-mail.

Costs such as for paper and pens are minimal and are better thought of as monthly expenses. Items such as a cell phone and a pager aren't immediately necessary. You can wait to see how your business evolves, and then decide whether these devices would be helpful.

A scanner is included on the high-end list because, in conjunction with your laser printer, it can be used as a part-time copier (as well as for other tasks). The fact that a scanner does not have a feeder for putting in more than one page at a time makes it cumbersome for copying large documents.

Ouch! That Hurts!

While you're shopping for office equipment, be sure you take your health into consideration. When we think of on-the-job injuries, we assume the types of jobs that cause them are those that require physical labor. Not so. You're just as likely to injure yourself at your comfy desk job.

Repetitive-stress injuries are caused by doing the same thing over and over again. Typing and using your mouse can cause you injuries and put you and your business on the sidelines—sometimes permanently. Other problems, such as neck and back pain, can be caused by not having your workstation set up for comfort and support.

Aside from a few generic precautions you can take, such as staying in good physical shape, keeping your monitor at a comfortable height, and using a chair that doesn't cause you back pain, your best insurance against injury is to listen to your body. If you feel pain, try to find a solution that will alleviate it. Usually, it isn't hard to figure out what's causing it if you take a look at how you work and what hurts. Is your mouse hand bothering you? Try using a different mouse, a wrist rest, or a different type of input device altogether. Lower back pain? Try giving your back the support it needs.

> **Smart Tip**
> The decision you make about whether to work at home or rent an office will have a big impact on your start-up expenses. If you do rent office space, consider setting up in an executive suite in which tenants share office equipment and services.

▲

With a little ingenuity, many of the solutions to ending the pain you develop from earning your keep don't even have to cost anything. Before buying that $1,000 chair, try supporting your back using pillows or rolled-up towels. A few reams of paper or a couple of old phone books are great for adjusting the height of your monitor. If you're uncomfortable with low-tech solutions, experiment with them anyway so that you'll know what you'll need when you go shopping.

Equipment Expenses

Equipment	Low-End	High-End
Computer	$800[1]	$1,500[2]
All-in-one printer/fax/copier	$200	N/A
Laser printer	N/A	$500
Fax machine	N/A	$125
Scanner	$50	$200
Telephone	$50	$100
Phone line installation	two lines[3]: $150	two lines + DSL[4]: $510
Zip drive (included with computer)	$180	N/A
Tape backup	N/A	$250
Word processing software	$150	N/A
Spreadsheet software	$150	N/A
Office software suite[5]	N/A	$550
ISP start-up	$25	$25
Desk	N/A	$400
Ergonomic office chair	N/A	$200
Total	$1,755	$4,360

Notes:

1. 2.53GHz Pentium 4 processor, 30GB hard drive, 128MB RAM, 16X DVD-ROM, 17-inch monitor, network-ready. One-year parts and replacement warranty.

2. 3.06GHz Pentium 4 processor, 60GB hard drive, 1256MB RAM, 16X DVD-ROM, 19-inch monitor, built-in Zip drive, network-ready. Three-year, next-business-day, on-site warranty.

3. One line shared between fax and Internet access, one line for voice calls.

4. Voice line, fax line, DSL for Internet access (including modem).

5. Includes spreadsheet software, word processing software, database software, e-mail software, and contact manager.

Dollar Stretcher

If you use a credit card to buy your equipment or for other business expenses, shop around for one that gives frequent-flier miles. Those miles can add up quickly when you're making your initial purchases, and they can take the sting out of laying out all that money.

A ton of information is available in books and magazines and on the Web for setting up a workstation that will help you avoid physical problems. But the fact is, what works for one person does not always work for another. What is important is that you take pain seriously, however minor it may seem. Figure out what is causing it if you can, and see a doctor if it lasts more than a week. Taking frequent breaks and stretching is a good way to stay healthy (you do not have a problem with taking breaks, right?). As an information consultant, you use your mind to make your money; but do not neglect your body when you're setting up your office.

To get a better idea of what your total start-up expenses will be, including office furniture, computer hardware and software, and the other equipment we have discussed, see "Start-Up Costs" on page 67.

Ongoing Costs

The monthly expenses for an information consultant are really pretty minimal compared to other types of businesses. Assuming you're working at home, expect your electric bill to increase by about $25 per month from running your office machines. Your ISP will charge around $25 per month for unlimited Web access and e-mail. Throw in paper for your fax machine and consumables for your printer, and you're looking at about another $15 per month. Mailing and copying costs may run another $25, as may auto expenses. Each phone line will cost you about $25 per month. So without including long-distance phone calls and high-speed Internet access, you can expect to pay under $200 per month in expenses. With cable modem or DSL access included, it comes to under $250 per month.

Depending on where your clients and other people you need to contact are located, your phone bill can sometimes be a frightening surprise. Keep an eye on it. Send faxes at the least expensive times of day (some fax machines have this feature built in), and bill your clients for any long-distance calls you make on their

Dollar Stretcher

The amount of paper you use can really add up. You can save money on paper by printing on both sides. Obviously, this won't work for reports you're sending out to clients, but it's just fine for day-to-day tasks like printing out e-mail or Web pages. Using the paper twice is good for the environment, too.

behalf. You may also want to shop around for the least expensive long-distance service available in your area. The difference between 7 cents a minute and 10 cents a minute may seem small, but it really adds up if you spend a lot of time with the phone attached to your ear. Some long-distance companies offer perks like frequent-flier miles that can make them even more attractive. You have to take a vacation sometime, don't you?

The Big Question: How Much Does It Pay?

The amount of money you make as an information consultant depends a lot on the amount of experience you have and the quality of your work. Other factors, such as the affluence of your clients and whether you're confident enough to ask for what you're worth, also come into play. You can't get blood from a turnip, and you can't sell services to people and companies who can't afford them. Before we dig any deeper into the mysteries of getting paid for the work you do, let's dispel one myth you'll hear repeatedly from clients in your role as an information consultant: "But it's all on the Web!" You'll hear this frequently, usually right after quoting your rates and generally from potential clients who have never used the services of an information consultant. These people don't yet have a clear idea of your value. Fear not. Whatever your rates happen to be, you don't need to be intimidated by a prospective client's assumption that the information he or she is requesting will be easy to find.

First off, it's usually not all on the Web. But even if it is, you can find the information and get the job done much faster than someone who doesn't have the same research skills you do. Second, as you'll soon find out, it's extremely rare to find all the information you're looking for on the Internet. Even if you do find most of what you're looking for, you'll have to check facts, talk to people on the phone, and generally fill in the blanks that aren't posted online.

Some types of research are best done on the Internet, some are best done using other online databases, and some will require you to be adept at using your local library. You'll find out that some research projects may have few (or no) electronic resources for you to rely on and may instead require that you talk to experts or get statistical information from government institutions. The nature of the beast

> ## Smart Tip
> Tip...
>
> Subcontracting work from experienced consultants can give you a better idea of what your work is worth. They've been around and will probably even tell you how much time they expect you to spend on a project, which will help you figure out if you're up to speed. Subcontracting work to contractors is another way to figure out how much time a project should take and what the work is worth from an hourly perspective.

determines the means to defeat it. And your arsenal of skills, which will develop over time, will make you a far more effective researcher than people who don't live and breathe the art of gathering information.

If prospective clients brush you aside, saying they could get the information off the Web themselves if they had the time, politely tell them you'll still be available if they change their mind. Often, these same people will try, realize the difficulties, and then call to secure your services.

Charging Ahead: Figuring Your Hourly Worth

There's really no set pricing for information consultants. Figuring out what to charge is something you'll get a feel for with time, but even then you'll occasionally underbid a job and have to work your butt off for less than your services are worth or overbid a job and not get it at all. The former situation, by the way, is far more painful than the latter. If you overbid and don't get a job, you can get right back on the horse and look for other work. If you underbid a job, you can end up having a project drag on and on while you wear yourself out working nights and weekends, watching your savings dwindle. As you gain more experience, you'll eventually reach a point where these situations will occur less frequently.

Joining an organization like the AIIP can be a tremendous help in figuring out how much your work is worth because becoming a member gives you access to consultants who have years of experience. Depending on your skills as a researcher and your knowledge of the field you'll be serving, you may decide to work as a subcontractor while you get a feel for how much to charge. That disclaimer aside, we'll hazard some estimates of what the pay is like by profiling information consultants at different skill levels:

- *$25 to 30 per hour.* You're just starting out and haven't worked in an information-gathering field before. You're either working part-time while you hold on to your day job or you have some other means of financial support. You've picked up some of the research skills you need by taking classes, or you're using skills you have from previous jobs. You feel comfortable searching for information on the Web but aren't an expert. You're primarily looking for subcontracting jobs where you are doing work for someone who is already established in the field.

- *$50 per hour.* You've become an expert at conducting Web searches and are

 Beware!
You should always have some type of written agreement for the work that you do. If you are doing work for a client who is basing financial decisions on your findings, it's especially important to have a lawyer check out your contract to be sure you won't be financially liable if you make a mistake.

comfortable but not yet an expert at finding information using online databases. You've proven yourself by subcontracting work from others and are beginning to get work on your own. If you were doing information consulting part-time, you're now getting enough work to quit your day job. This pay rate is also the starting point for consultants who have worked as librarians or researchers but are just beginning to work independently.

- *$75 per hour.* You are now getting enough work on your own that you are doing little or no subcontracting unless it's because other consultants are hiring you for your knowledge in a specific field— and then only accepting projects when you can make close to your standard pay rate. You are comfortable with Web searching, database searching, and telephone interviews, or you know your own

skills well enough to begin subcontracting work outside your area of expertise to others. You haven't had to seek out work in six months to a year, and you have more than one regular client.

- *$100 per hour.* Besides the skills you had at the previous pay level, you are becoming well known as an expert in the industry you serve. You are probably being asked to speak at conventions and write articles for magazines. You have enough work to confidently subcontract certain tasks to others—mostly because you have worked with enough subcontractors to know whom to trust.

- *$150 and up.* You are an expert in the field you serve as well as an expert in information consulting. You are being asked to not only find information for clients, but to consult with them to help them figure out what questions they need answers to, and why. You are a frequent speaker at conventions, contributor to magazines, or author of books, either about the subject you specialize in or about information consulting itself. You may be training others or giving seminars about the skills you've gained as an information consultant. You probably analyze the data you gather for your clients and may even go on-site to present the information.

All of the hourly rates we've listed are estimates and can be affected by many factors. Maybe you were already working as a researcher for a large corporation and left

> **Beware!**
> Even though you have a contract with a client, there may be times when you end up not getting paid. Some companies, unfortunately, are just deadbeats. Really, your only recourse in a situation where a client won't pay is not to work for that client again. The amount you would be paid for a single job generally doesn't make it worthwhile to hire a lawyer. Small-claims court is an option if you have the time and energy. In either case, by now you've realized you won't work with these folks again anyway.

your job while continuing to serve that corporation as an independent consultant. Or maybe you are already an expert in a particular field and will be looking for clients among people who already have a lot of respect for your skills. Perhaps you were a librarian. Any of these factors will increase the amount you should be charging for your services. The amount you earn will be affected not only by your skills, but also by what the market will bear in the field you serve.

Making the Bid: Flat Rate or Hourly?

This question is not really as scary as it sounds if you take the time to think about each job and protect yourself with a contract. Clients know how much they can spend to acquire your services. Whether you charge an hourly rate or a flat rate, you can't expect to be compensated adequately by clients who can't afford your fees. For example, if a client has $3,000 to spend and your rate is $100 an hour, you need to be able to get the work done in 30 hours to satisfy the client. If your rate is $50 an hour, you need to be able to get it done in 60 hours. The problem is that the client, trying to remain within or below budget, is not going to tell you how much he or she has to spend.

Here's where you need to be honest with yourself about your capabilities. Review what is required of you to complete the work, and make an honest estimate of the number of hours it will take you. Because most of us are extremely optimistic that we won't run into any snags along the way, we tend to shortchange ourselves, so add at least 50 percent to your estimated hours (some consultants double their estimates to be safe) and bid based on that number. The fact is, there isn't much difference between charging a flat rate and charging an hourly rate. Even if you bid hourly, the client will generally ask you how many hours it will take to complete a job.

If you are asked to make a flat-rate bid, make sure you have a written agreement that states what you're expected to do. Also explain in writing that if the job goes beyond the description you and the client have agreed on, you will have to charge hourly for the overrun. If you need to charge for overrun, however, be sure to notify the client in advance that the project is going to cost more money. You should also be sure there is a really good reason that it's taking longer to complete the job. If the job is taking longer because you didn't estimate the hours correctly, you may decide that you don't want to charge for the extra work—so that you can keep the client. Drastically inaccurate time estimates followed by major cost overruns can make it appear that you bid low to get the job, knowing it would take you much longer to complete (and cost the client's company much more than it planned to spend).

Whether flat or hourly, your rates should be based on your capabilities. Don't be tempted to underbid just to get a job. If the client decides not to hire you based on a reasonable bid, walk away and look for other work.

Billing

Here's the fun part—payday. You can bill the client immediately after the work is completed to their satisfaction. Be sure to charge for online database access, long-distance phone calls on the client's behalf, and your hourly or flat rate. Your monthly ISP charge is counted as one of your business expenses because you also use it for e-mail and personal Web access. Putting a note on the invoice that says "Payment due in 15 (or 30) days" gives you a set time after which to call the client if you haven't received your payment. (See the sample invoice below.)

Other scenarios will require you to make financial arrangements with the client before starting the job. For example, if a job is going to continue for an extended period of time, you may want to make arrangements to send the client an invoice once a month. Some information consultants also work on a retainer fee just like lawyers. They are paid once a month to be available to the client for a specified maximum

---

Invoice

To: Bob N. Frapples
        Grandma Frapples' Snappy Apple Pies
        5201 Golden Delicious St., #151
        McIntosh, WA 98100

From: Jane Doe
        Doe Information Services

Service: Contracted research on the apple pie industry
(2/1/04 through 3/6/04)

Research charge	40 hrs @ $50 per hr	$2,000.00
Online database charges	20 hrs @ $25 per hr	$500.00
Document retrieval (*New York Times*)	10 @ $1.35	$13.50
Long-distance phone charges		$75.00
(for interviews; see attached copy of phone bill)		
	Total:	$2,588.50

Payment is due within 30 days. Please make check payable to:
Doe Information Services
321 Data St.
Research, CA 94100
(415) 555-3888
(415) 555-8388 (fax)

---

number of hours, whether or not they actually do any work. In this case, depending on your agreement and contract, you may not even need to send an invoice.

Expected Annual Income

If you skipped the preceding sections and jumped straight to this section, go to the back of the class. There are a zillion different factors that will affect how much you make in a year as an information consultant, and they run the gamut from experience and skill to the type of information you're gathering. It should be pretty obvious that some types of companies, such as big-name law firms and large high-tech companies, probably have more money to spend on information than, say, your local plumbers' union.

That said, an information consultant in the $50-per-hour range can make about $40,000 a year. The top salaries will be earned by those who are considered experts in their information fields—those who write articles, speak at conferences, and consult. These experts bring in anywhere from $100,000 a year on up, depending on the

---

Start-Up Costs

Here's a list of the average start-up costs for an information consultant who's working from a home office (which is usually the case). Because it's assumed that you will be starting out from the comfort of your home, this list of expenses does not include office space or equipment for additional employees. The costs shown are estimates based on reasonable expenditures for computer equipment, furniture, and the like. For example, if you're buying a $1,500 computer and spending $2,000 for a Chippendale desk and chair, your expenses will be higher. If you're using a computer you already own and an old kitchen table for a desk, your costs will be significantly lower. Use the "Start-Up Costs Worksheet" on page 68 to figure out your actual costs.

Items	Prices
Office furniture	$350
Computer hardware	$1,500
Computer software	$700
Phone and fax machine	$200
Printed collateral (business cards, letterhead stationery)	$100
Phone line installation (two lines)	$150
Other communication devices (cell phone, pager)	$100
Miscellaneous expenses (Add about 10% of total)	$360
Total Start-Up Costs	**$3,460**

length of time they've been in the business (the longer they've worked as information consultants, the bigger their base of regular clients).

One more thing to keep in mind before multiplying your hourly rate by 40 hours a week is that a lot of the work you do, including bookkeeping, studying, attending conferences, and looking for work, is stuff you don't get paid for—and can be pretty time-consuming, to boot. Being an information consultant takes a lot of work. The work is rewarding and pays well, but it's definitely not for those looking for a get-rich-quick scheme.

Start-Up Costs Worksheet

Items	Prices
Office furniture	$_____
Computer hardware	_____
Computer software	_____
Phone and fax machine	_____
Printed collateral (business cards, letterhead stationery)	_____
Phone line installation (at least two lines)	_____
Other communication devices (cell phone, pager)	_____
Miscellaneous expenses (Add about 10% of total.)	_____
Total Start-Up Costs	$_____

What Do You Want to Know Today?

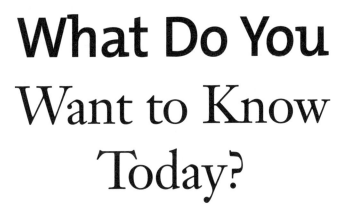

Although locating information is obviously the most important part of the information consultant's job, the means by which this elusive information can be found are not nearly as obvious. At first glance, it might seem that you could merely log on to the Web, do a quick search, deliver the information to the client, and send out an invoice. But gathering information is not as simple as it seems. (If it were, you would not have a job.) The Web, while a tremendous resource, is not the pot of gold at the end of the rainbow. Information—even if it is posted by a company you're researching—must be verified. Finding absolutely every stitch of information you're looking for on the Web is a pipe dream at best. However, even if the data you're looking for isn't right there to be pulled up on your monitor, the contacts who can give you the information usually are. In most cases, you'll find one or the other—both if you're lucky—but you'll still need to make calls to verify the information. (You're not looking for total isolation, are you?)

In this chapter, we'll look at using the Internet for research. Keep in mind that the Web is not the only source of information online. Information consultants also use online databases, some of which are complex enough that you need to take a class to learn how to use them. (We'll discuss online databases in this chapter as well.) The Web is used as an example to show how to logically put together a search. Depending on the subject you're researching, you may have to use other resources.

Focusing Your Search

The quantity of information available is so vast that you need to help your clients find out precisely what they want so that you can narrow the parameters of your search. This can be tricky, especially if you're hired at an hourly rate. Why would you want to narrow your search when more hours equal more money? Well, the quality of the information you provide is almost always more important than the quantity. If you work fewer hours and get your clients exactly what they're looking for, chances are they'll call you the next time they need help. It's important to explain to clients that you're not trying to make less work for yourself, but rather trying to pinpoint exactly what they need.

As any experienced information consultant will tell you, clients almost always initially look for the quantity of information you can provide, regardless of whether that mass of knowledge is what they actually need. If you take what clients initially ask you for at face value without helping them focus on what they actually need, neither of you will be happy. Part of your job is to help your clients identify what they really want to learn. If you hold a focusing session for free before deciding to take a job, it will save you and your clients a large investment in aspirin.

Here's a hypothetical scenario that will show you how to help clients define exactly what information they are looking for. Bob N. Frapples, president of Grandma Frapples' Snappy Apple Pies, calls you on the phone and tells you he will pay you $10,000 to spend a month finding out absolutely everything about apples. As a

> **Tip...**
>
> **Smart Tip**
>
> Try to find out not only what your clients want you to research but also why they want the information. This will allow you to add value to your final product by gathering extra information that your clients might be able to use.

savvy information consultant who specializes in produce, you're tempted to jump on the offer—this being substantially higher than your usual rate. Now stop for a second and think. At the end of the job, you will have compiled every bit of information that's available on apples, and you'll turn it over to Big Bob.

Is that what he really wants? Probably not. You ran into this same situation last year with the Oranjello's World-Famous Orange Juice contract. Sure, you got paid (lucky thing, too). But you heard through the grapevine that Mrs. Oranjello, the president of the company, was so disappointed with your work that she hired another consultant. This other consultant realized that Mrs. Oranjello really wanted to

Smart Tip

Tip...

When you go on-site to meet clients, always dress for success. While many companies have adopted casual dress codes, there's nothing more disconcerting than walking into a room full of suits dressed like you just dropped by on your way to the grocery store. Being a little overdressed is better than being underdressed. You can change back into jeans and a T-shirt when you get home.

find information on a particularly sweet strain of oranges grown using environmentally friendly methods, in an effort to appeal to the politically correct orange juice drinkers in the San Francisco market.

You schedule a meeting with Mr. Frapples. Now it's your job to be sure that both you and Big Bob know what you're looking for. First, Bob wonders why you wanted to meet him. Finding out everything about apples seems pretty straightforward—especially for what he's paying you. You explain that knowing more about why he wants this information will help you find exactly what he needs. (You'll also detail the results of this meeting in your contract to protect yourself.)

Here's what you find out. One of Bob's competitors is crushing him in the marketplace with a special variety of apples that costs less and tastes better than his. The competing company makes better-tasting apple pies at a third of the cost. Bob wants apples in his pies that taste just as good and lower his costs to a competitive level, but they can't be used in anyone else's pies.

A few questions later, you find out that it doesn't matter whether some other company is using the apples he'll use, as long as it isn't a national company that competes with his company and his chief competitor. In fact, if there's a promising independent bakery that only serves a small market, he might even be interested in buying it out and using its apple pie recipe—as long as the company doesn't use the same apples his chief competitor uses, and the apples used in its recipe lower his costs. He'd also like to know whether the company's pies are popular.

That's a far cry from melting your brain, trying to find out absolutely everything about apples. You now have clues that will help you find the information Bob needs. You draw up a contract and take the job.

The Cheat Sheet

Before you look for any information on the Web, you need to simplify it into even more basic terms than you received from the client. Why? Computers and computer systems are not intelligent. While the creators of search engines and other types of software may want you to believe their programs are "intuitive," the fact is, you're putting information into a machine and asking it to sort it the way you want it sorted. Your computer can't read your mind any better than you would have been able to read the mind of Bob N. Frapples based on his first phone call. A computer is kind of like a really powerful pocket calculator. If you hit the wrong keys, you can't possibly expect to get the correct answer. A common saying among computer programmers is "Garbage in, garbage out," meaning that the value of the information that comes out of a program is directly related to the accuracy of the data put in.

Let's get back to our example of the Grandma Frapples' Snappy Apple Pies job. Before you begin your research, narrow what you're looking for down to the simplest possible terms. List every piece of information you're looking for, then try to pare it down to a couple of sentences. What you're trying to do here is come up with a couple of short phrases that you can type into your computer—because it's just not smart enough to deal with much more.

What does Mr. Frapples want to know? Well, we'll call his competitor's apples "Gunkos" for this little exercise, and the apples he's currently using "Frumpos." Mr. Frapples wants to find:

- Apples that are used in apple pies, but not Gunko apples or Frumpo apples.
- Apple pie bakeries that use neither Gunko apples nor Frumpo apples and aren't national companies but make popular pies.

We'll need to narrow this down more later, but that's a good start. Now before you turn on the computer, brainstorm for a moment about the places you're most likely to find this information—not specific Web sites, just logically. Apples used in apple pies could be found in recipes, for example. Information about apple prices might be available from apple orchards.

You also want to find bakeries that produce popular apple pies. The popularity of the bakeries' pies can be expressed in a couple of ways. You might dig up financial information about the companies. You might also find statements like "Chicago's most popular apple pies" or "Baking apple

Bright Idea

Before you take on any jobs as an information consultant, hone your Web searching skills by doing research on topics you're interested in. Make the information you are looking for as specific as possible. For example, don't just research "dogs." Try to find out the health problems that are most likely to affect English bulldogs living in Arizona.

pies for over 50 years" on the companies' Web sites. Because you're searching the Web for small, privately owned bakeries, you'll probably be looking for descriptive statements rather than financial information. Financial information about publicly traded companies is a lot easier to find because they have to send reports to the federal government and those reports are available on the Web. However, information about privately owned companies can sometimes be found by searching newspaper archives online. Such articles often give sales figures. Remember, the client didn't specifically ask you for financial information. You're just trying to determine the popularity of the pies.

Start Your Engine

Now you're ready to begin your search. We'll start with a little background on the capabilities of search engines. There's an ongoing debate among Internet users about which is the best. A search engine is a software program that allows you to type in words

E-Search Shortcuts

There are a number of places to start looking for information that may give you a head start on your Internet research:

- ○ *Magazines.* Nearly every field you can think of is served by an industry magazine. Many of these magazines publish annual resource lists or background articles that you can purchase as back issues. Most magazines now have Web sites, many of which list back issues and their tables of contents.
- ○ *Industry organizations.* Just about every field has a professional organization of some sort. Find the list of members, and you've also found a valuable list of contacts for your research. Many organizations have Web sites with links to their members' home pages.
- ○ *Standards organizations.* If you're researching a topic that is governed by standards, whether they are self-imposed or government-imposed, the Web site for the standards organization will most likely have a list of the companies that comply. Just as with industry organizations, these Web sites provide valuable contact information and may feature links to member companies' sites.
- ○ *Government listings.* The U.S. government has approximately 12,600 Web sites that list everything from corporate financial reports to patent records. Links to many of the most frequently used sites can be found at the official Web portal, www.firstgov.gov.

Smart Tip

Tip...

In both Microsoft Internet Explorer and Netscape Navigator, you can speed up your Web access by telling the program not to display pictures or animations. To use this option in Internet Explorer, uncheck the Show Pictures box (choose View in the menu bar, scroll down to Internet Options and click, then choose the Advanced tab). In Netscape, just uncheck the box that says Automatically Load Images (to find this, click on Edit in the menu bar, choose Preferences, then click on Advanced).

---

for it to find in the content of Web pages around the world. AltaVista (www.altavista.com) is a good pick for information consultants for a few reasons. First, it allows you to search Web pages posted in the United States or worldwide, and in a specific language, or in English and/or Spanish. More important, it allows you to do a Boolean search, which we'll describe in detail shortly.

This is not intended to discount any of the other popular search engines. Some have all these features, and some have other features that may be attractive for different reasons. "Meta-search" engines such as Dogpile (www.dogpile.com) allow you to search more than a dozen search engines at a time. Google has also become extremely popular for its up-to-date search technologies (www.google.com).

Not all search engines update their listings the same way. You can do the exact same search on three search engines and get three different listings of Web pages that match the criteria you've entered. This can be useful during your research. After you've mastered one search engine, experiment with others until you find another one you're comfortable with. Then switch between the two during your searches to see if you get different results.

The Mathematics of Words

The reason you should put your logic cap on before doing a Web search is that computers and search engines don't really understand the words you're typing in. They are simply looking at a string of characters and trying to locate those same characters in Web pages. For example, if you type in the word apple, the search engine doesn't know whether you intend to bake a pie or buy a computer. You need a way to better explain what you're looking for so that the search engine can list Web sites that have the information you need.

Most search engines allow you to specify relationships between the words you're typing in very simple ways—for example, using a plus sign to show that you are looking to find two words, e.g., *apple + pie*. Some even offer buttons you can click on to specify whether you're looking for listings with "any of the words" or "all of the words" that you've typed in. The methods for indicating relationships among the words you're seeking vary, depending on the search engine you're using.

Nearly all search engines, however, offer much more powerful tools for searching called Boolean operators. The Boolean search is named after George Boole, a 19th-century

British mathematician who came up with the idea that logical thought could be expressed as algebraic sequences. In terms of working with computers, this idea makes a lot of sense because they are maddeningly logical devices.

A Boolean expression is like a mathematical expression that uses words or symbols between the words you are hunting for to indicate relationships between or among them. For example, if you want to search for *apple pie* but not *Apple computers*, you can use the Boolean search option and key in: *apple AND pie AND NOT computer.* This will generate a list of Web pages that contain the words *apple* and *pie* (somewhere on the same Web page, but not necessarily right next to each other) but not the word *computer* (even if the page contains the words *apple* and *pie*). Here's a list of the Boolean operators that are used in the AltaVista search engine:

> ## ⚠ Beware!
> Many a researcher has made the mistake of spending too much time following useless leads on the Web. If you get more than a couple hundred listings, you have thrown your net too wide and are wasting valuable time. Excessive listings (also called "hits") are an indication that you haven't defined your search well enough.

- *AND.* Finds only documents containing all of the specified words or phrases. *Mary* AND *lamb* finds documents with both the word *Mary* and the word *lamb.*

- *OR.* Finds documents containing at least one of the specified words or phrases. *Mary* OR *lamb* finds documents containing either *Mary* or *lamb.* The found documents could contain both, but do not have to.

- *NOT.* Excludes documents containing the specified word or phrase. *Mary* AND NOT *lamb* finds documents containing *Mary* but not *lamb.* NOT cannot stand alone. It must be used with another operator, such as AND.

- *NEAR.* Finds documents containing both specified words or phrases within 10 words of each other. *Mary* NEAR *lamb* would most likely find the nursery rhyme.

altaVista: Search   Live!   Shopping   Raging Bull   Free Internet Access   Email

| Search | Advanced Search | Images | MP3/Audio | Video |

Boolean query: [ ]   **Search**
- Advanced Search Help
- Advanced Search Tutorial
- Family Filter is **off**
- Language Settings

Advanced Search Cheat Sheet

Sort by: [ ]

Language: [any language ⬍]   ☐ Show one result per Web site

From: [ ]   **To:** [ ]   (e.g. 31/12/99)

▲

Bright Idea

Not every Web address ends in ".com." The letters at the end of addresses have meanings that may help you make quicker sense of the results you get when you use a search engine. Addresses that end in ".edu" are educational institutions like colleges. Those that end in ".org" are organizations, and addresses that end in ".gov" are run by federal and state government agencies. New top-level extensions include .biz and .info. Countries also have their own Web address endings: ".uk" is the United Kingdom, ".ca" is Canada, and ".fi" is Finland.

To find Web pages that have the word *apple* within ten words of the word *pie* but don't have the word *computer* or the words *gunko* or *frumpo*, you would enter: *apple NEAR pie AND NOT computer AND NOT gunko AND NOT frumpo*.

In a Boolean search, phrases should be placed in parentheses. For example, if you want to find the exact phrase *apple pie*, rather than using *apple NEAR pie*, which will list the Web pages that have those two words within 10 words of each other, you would use (*apple pie*), which will find Web pages that have the words right next to each other.

One more tip: Use lowercase for the words you want unless you specifically want to find the word in the form you typed it. Typing *apple* in lowercase gives you any form of the word, no matter how it appears (*Apple, APPLE, aPPle*, you get the idea). Typing in *Apple* will only give you Web pages that have the word exactly as typed, with a capital "A" followed by lowercase letters.

The Right Tools for the Job

The topic of how best to get information comes up constantly in discussions among information consultants. Many are devout users of online, pay-as-you-go databases. Others are devotees of primary research who insist on contacting people directly by phone.

Carole L., an information specialist in Vista, California, was able to shed some light on how information consultants gather data. "I use all the methods that are available. I use the Internet a lot today. Certainly there are projects I can do just on the Web, but if the client wants analyst opinions about whether this is a good product or what their competitors think about them, I'm going to pick up the phone, and I'm going to use services like Dialog or LexisNexis. People hire you to find an answer, so you've got to have all your tools in your toolbox. The more tools you're fluent with, the better job you can do for your client."

You can use Boolean terms to narrow the number of Web site listings the search engine returns until you get the information you want. The trick here is to know what you want to find and how to communicate your needs to the search engine. (Now you can probably see why you needed to take a little time to clarify exactly what you were looking for before booting up your computer.)

Boolean searches are possible with most search engines, and each search engine has its own strengths and weaknesses. Try mastering one search engine at a time until you find the one that's right for you. Most information consultants use different engines for different purposes to get the most out of the World Wide Web.

Just the Facts

You'll rarely find all the information you need on your first search, and sometimes you won't find much more than a phone number or an address. But this information is still very valuable. Even if it looks like you've found all the information you were looking for, you need to gather contact information from all the Web pages you visit. Why? Like any other information medium, the Internet can contain inaccuracies, which you definitely don't want to pass on to your clients. And most Web pages have disclaimers at the bottom, shirking responsibility for errors.

Here's where you run into the Catch-22 of having all this information at your disposal. If you have to call the sources to verify what's on their Web sites, why not just call them in the first place and have them provide the information? Well, if you call for information, you'll most likely be referred to a Web site that supposedly has everything you need. It's best to get as much content as you can from the Web site, and then call to verify that information and fill in anything that wasn't available online. If you make a habit of copying contact info as you go, it'll be much easier to go down the list of contacts. You'll also be able to refer to a specific person with whom you spoke or exchanged e-mail, should any questions come up about the accuracy of the information.

Most Web sites have at least one contact person listed, usually the Webmaster, whom you can get in touch with to find out who can verify the information you gathered. Some sites list contact information for everyone in the company or organization. Be careful and thorough when you check your facts. Inaccurate information not only causes you to lose clients, but can also bring you legal problems, depending on the field you're researching.

Tip...

Smart Tip

If you know the name of a specific company and you want to find its Web page, try typing the company's name in the address line of your Web browser in this format: www.companyname.com. Most companies try to make finding them on the Web as easy as possible. Many new companies now even choose their names based on the availability of corresponding Web addresses.

▲

Less Obvious Online Resources

Sometimes, being a little creative in your research efforts can really pay off. Earlier in this chapter, we put together a cheat sheet to figure out how to logically search for the information we sought. Well, doing some additional brainwork upfront can save you even more time. There may be organizations or industry magazines that serve the field you are researching. Sometimes you may even find that someone else has done research on a topic similar to yours. Information from these sources is often available online free of charge for you to use as a starting point. Other times, you may decide that it's worth shelling out a few bucks to buy a report or back issues of a magazine to give yourself a head start.

In the case of our research job for Bob N. Frapples, we found a listing of apple growers' associations. Sadly, all their members grow either Frumpo or Gunko apples. But we did get a ton of contact information for apple growers, whom we can call to ask questions and get leads on where we might find pricing information and maybe even recipes. We also found an industry report called *Bakery Production & Marketing* that might be helpful. We just need to call the company that produces the report to find out what it contains. If it has information that could save us a couple of days of research, like listings of bakeries in the United States, it might be worth purchasing.

You're It! Avoiding Phone Tag

The cheapest way to verify information you've found on the Web is via e-mail. Most Web sites will have some sort of e-mail contact posted. However, e-mail is not the most effective way to get a quick response. Phone calls are often faster, but they can be expensive during business hours if you need to contact a large number of people.

Try using a two-pronged approach to get a quicker response. Put together your list of e-mail contacts and your list of phone contacts for the same companies (assuming you've found both). Send out all your e-mail requests on a Friday afternoon after business hours. Then on Friday night or over the weekend (whichever is the cheaper long-distance rate), call and leave each contact a voice-mail message letting him or her know that you sent an e-mail message to verify information. On Monday morning, all the people you contacted will get both e-mail and voice mail from you. You'll get a much higher response than if you used only one of the two contact methods. (And you won't be interrupting those few people who still answer their phones during business hours.)

Online Databases

Online databases, some of which date back to the early 1960s, can also be useful in tracking down data. Some information consultants use online databases almost exclusively, depending on their field of research. For example, Dialog has databases of information about chemistry, biomedicine, pharmaceuticals, engineering, and technology. LexisNexis has databases that cover legal and government issues, as well as business and technology. Factiva, a joint venture of Dow Jones & Co. and Reuters, has news articles from nearly 8,000 different sources, including *The Wall Street Journal* and more than 900 non-English publications and Web sites. Other databases cater to particular subjects, such as medical information or legal decisions.

Online databases charge in a variety of ways, including annual subscriptions, hourly charges, search fees, connection charges, and download fees. Subscription fees range from $200 to $1,000, depending on the database. Fortunately, some of them offer discounts to information consultants who are members of professional organizations like the AIIP.

If a database is available that provides information on the specific field you're working in, it can be an invaluable resource. Unfortunately, specialized online databases can be difficult to navigate because each requires that you use a slightly different search language to find the information you need. Many online databases date back to before the age of the Internet and can still be accessed by a direct (non-Internet) dial-in connection, but most of them have moved to the Internet. As they become more available to the masses, they may also become easier to use.

If the industry you serve requires you to access pay-per-hour online databases—for example, if you need to access databases of patent information about pharmaceutical products—don't waste your time and money trying to teach yourself how to use them. Many companies and experienced individuals offer workshops at affordable prices. The AIIP has an annual conference where you can attend classes that will help you get the skills you need. Some professional information consultants also can be hired as mentors to teach you personally. Check out the AIIP's Web site for more information.

Being Your Own Best Resource

One of the most important resources you'll have will be a database or (at the very least) a list of all the information you've ever researched. Save absolutely every bit of information you gather. If a new client calls and asks you to do research that is similar to something you've done before, you'll be five steps ahead. Project overlap is bound to happen when you're conducting research in the same field. Doing good work will help you build a reputation as an expert. The more jobs you do, the larger your own database of information will become. Remember, the computer is just one of the tools you use to find information. The most important tool at your disposal is the ability to think logically. Your clients may not know it, but that's what they're really paying you for.

Presentation Methods

Once you've gathered all the information your client has requested, how do you go about presenting it? There really isn't a standard format in which to present the information your research turns up. Your final report should obviously be readable, and it should answer the questions your client wanted answered. But how you present the data depends completely on your client's needs, which you will have to adapt to on the fly at first. Some clients want spreadsheets; some want bound reports; some prefer Microsoft Word files; some ask for information in the form of an Access, File-Maker, or other database file; and some want PowerPoint presentations.

Smart Tip

Knowing how to present data is a skill in itself. Information consultants who aren't especially good at organizing data often prefer to hire others to put together printed reports or slide presentations. Likewise, more than a few information consultants with strong data-presentation skills offer database development services in which they organize clients' existing data into a searchable format for easy use.

Providing your timely, well-researched data in a format the client can't read isn't going to score you any points and can even prove embarrassing. If you're not good at desktop publishing or working with databases, or if the client asks for the information to be delivered in a format you're not skilled in, try to find another information consultant (or software expert) to whom you can subcontract the creation of the report. If this situation occurs more often than you're comfortable with, it may be time to take a few classes to get up to speed.

Good Exposure
Promoting Your Business

How do you let potential clients know that you exist? Welcome to the wonderful world of advertising. If you're an independent information consultant, it's quite possible that you walked away from your previous place of work with a potential client—maybe even your former employer if you played your cards right. However, even if you come out of

▲

the chute with one or two clients, it's unlikely that they will bring in enough work for you to rest on your laurels and wait for them to call every week. You need exposure.

In this chapter, we look at some of the ways you can get your name out there so that people will know who you are and what you have to offer. Before we get started, you'll need to do a little bit of work. Figure out what industry would be most interested in your services. Next, compile a list of companies in that field, along with contact information for the person in each company who is most likely to need your services. If you are a legal researcher, you'll need a list of law firms and contacts. If you are a high-tech researcher, you'll need a list of software and hardware companies.

Because there are so many fields in which information consultants provide services, you are pretty much on your own in finding an initial list of potential clients. Do some research. Leaf through magazines. Click around on the Web. Even flip through the Yellow Pages if you think that's where the information lies. Still no list of clients? Not to worry. The following marketing ideas should help you find those first clients.

It's in the Cards

Ah, the lowly business card. It's an often overlooked but extremely effective marketing tool. It's also just about the cheapest form of marketing you can do. For about $50 to $60, you can have enough business cards printed to last you a year, so go ahead and get them printed professionally at your local copy shop instead of trying to print them yourself on those sheets of perforated paper bought at the office supply store. It is such a small expense that it does not make sense to be perceived as unprofessional by potential clients in the name of frugality here. A sloppy business card is as bad as a sloppy resume. Having a professional-looking business card, on the other hand, makes your business look like it means business. Keep your card simple. Be sure to include your phone and fax numbers, e-mail address, and Web site address (if you have one). If you work out of your apartment, you might consider using "Suite 340" instead of "Apt. 340." Most information consultants will tell you that a homebased business usually appears less legitimate to clients than a business run out of a suite in an office building. It's all about perception.

Business cards are extremely important, so you should carry yours with you at all times. You need them in any situation where you might bump into potential clients. And the fact is, you could bump into a potential client just about anywhere, from the waiting room at the dentist's office to your local watering hole or even the airport. This is not to say that clients are going to fall out of the

Bright Idea

Information professionals aren't the only folks who join organizations. Find out what organizations your potential clients belong to and see if these groups have Web sites with lists of members to whom you can send your sales letters, press releases, and brochures.

sky and land in your lap. But if you happen to be talking to someone while you're waiting at the airport or in line at the movies, and you discover that the person is the CEO of a company you've been dying to take on as a client, you'll feel really silly if he or she asks for your card and you have to scramble for a scrap of paper and a pen to write down your information. (Carry a pen, too, in case you bump into that CEO and he or she is out of business cards—how unprofessional!)

Keeping professionalism in mind, you may also want to invest in things like letterhead stationery and envelopes. However, with the capabilities of most word processing programs, you can get around that expense by creating a template (a document that is blank except for information you want to have in every document of its type) that has your name at the top and your contact information at the bottom. If you use the same template and a good paper stock for all of your correspondence, it will look like you are using letterhead stationery.

While these kinds of printed products may seem like they fall into the category of office supplies, they're really marketing tools. You're trying to sell your services, so you need to live, eat, and breathe professionalism. Even when you are talking to potential clients on the telephone or meeting with them for lunch, you're marketing your business.

Snail Mail Potential

There are all sorts of nifty promotional pieces you can mail to potential clients, from simple sales letters to brochures. First off, as we said in the beginning of the chapter, you'll need to know what companies to mail them to. Getting information about companies in your field of expertise and finding out to whom exactly you should send printed materials are excellent exercises to sharpen your research skills before you actually go into business. Search the Web. Buy magazines. Go to libraries. Do everything you can to find out who and where your clients are. Got your list? OK, now let's take a look at what you can send potential clients.

Beware!
Don't be tempted to print out brochures on your inkjet printer. While there are companies that offer prefolded inkjet card stock designed for this purpose, brochures printed on this type of paper tend to look unprofessional. Worse, they make you look less than successful. "If your services are so great," your prospective clients will wonder, "Why can't you afford to have your brochures professionally printed?"

- *Sales letters.* Letters describing your services and your background are great, especially if you have other information to include with the letter, such as magazine articles you've written on a subject pertinent to the client (more on writing magazine articles later). Keep the letter brief and to the point, like the sample sales letter on page 84, and make it clear that you are an independent contractor. In other words, it should be clear to the client that you are not looking for a full-time position. (You don't want your information forwarded to the human resources department.) Make the letter as businesslike as possible and be sure to have a resume ready to send out if you're asked for it.

- *Press releases.* Everyone likes to keep up-to-date with his or her profession. So another effective way to get noticed is to send out press releases. You can't use information that you supply to clients in your press releases. But in the downtime between jobs or in the months before you start your business, you can do

---

Sales Letter

Doe Information Services

Information Is Power

321 Data St., Research, CA 94100 ◆ (415) 555-3888 ◆ Fax: (415) 555-8388 ◆ www.doeinfo.com

April 10, 200x

Michelle Appleton
Cobblers 'R' Us
425 Granny Smith Rd., Suite 201
Red Delicious, IL 60000

Dear Ms. Appleton,

After nearly 20 years in the field of agriculture, I have decided to start my own business providing much-needed information to the industry. My new venture, Doe Information Services, is a service that can provide your company with everything you need to know about the industry, from competitive intelligence to stock trends and end-user satisfaction (the consumers who eat your pies). I believe that my company's services can help your business and I invite you to contact me to discuss just what I can do for your company. My resume, which highlights my experience in agriculture, is attached.

Sincerely,

Jane Doe

Jane Doe, President
Doe Information Services

Press Release

Doe Information Services
Information Is Power
321 Data St., Research, CA 94100 ◆ (415) 555-3888 ◆ Fax: (415) 555-8388 ◆ www.doeinfo.com

FOR IMMEDIATE RELEASE

Contact: Jane Doe
(415) 555-3888, ext. 100, or janed@doeinfo.com

DOE INFORMATION SERVICES PREDICTS 25% INCREASE IN SWEET VERDE APPLE SALES

*Early winter in Northwest to blame for high price of Gunkos;
lower-priced alternative will lead to huge profits for growers.*

Research, CA—April 20, 2004—Doe Information Services, a leading information consulting firm in the field of agriculture, has predicted an unprecedented 25 percent increase in sales for a new strain of apples called Sweet Verdes. Sweet Verde apples, similar in taste and texture to America's favorite Gunko apples, were unveiled last year at the International Apple Consortium's annual conference in Bellevue, Washington.

"When Sweet Verde apples were first introduced, industry pundits were convinced sales would be weak due to their similarity to the famous Gunkos," said Jane Doe, president and CEO of Doe Information Services. "However, just as in real estate, the key difference was location." Due to an early winter and unprecedented snow in the Northwest, this year's crop of Gunko apples suffered a mortality rate of nearly 20 percent. Sweet Verde apples, on the other hand, are grown in Southern California and are widely available despite the bad weather in the North. The price of Gunkos has increased by 20 percent, prompting large consumer-oriented bakeries around the world to switch to Sweet Verdes, which are available at one-third the price currently asked for Gunkos.

"Switching to Sweet Verdes was a no-brainer for us," said Bob N. Frapples, CEO of Grandma Frapples' Snappy Apple Pies, which supplies nearly 20 percent of the apple pies consumed in the U.S. market. "The taste of the apples is virtually the same, and our tests show that some people actually prefer the taste of the Sweet Verdes. When prices go up, as they have for our competitors who are still using Gunkos, brand-name loyalty goes out the window."

Doe is also bullish on the stock price of Sweet Verde apples. "Doe Information Services predicts that the stock price of Sweet Verdes will increase 25 percent by year's end," she said in a recent interview.

About Doe Information Services
Doe Information Services is a full-service provider of analysis, competitive intelligence, and overall data for the agriculture industry.

▲

your own research and perhaps come up with key information and conclusions about the market you intend to serve.

You'll want to send press releases not only to potential clients, but also to magazines that are related to your area of expertise. There's a magazine that serves just about every professional market. If there isn't one serving yours, maybe you should start one (we'll leave that for another start-up guide). You should send press releases out on a regular basis—maybe once a month—at least until your business is up and prosperous. Be careful not to give away all your findings at once. (The sample press release on page 85 will give you some ideas about what kind of information to include.)

Besides sending your press releases to potential clients and industry publications, you may want to have them professionally distributed. For example, the Internet News Bureau (www.newsbureau.com) will e-mail your press release to more than a thousand online media outlets for about $275. It e-mails a newsletter to 6,000 subscribers. Comparable services are available to send press releases by snail mail. For more information about press releases, turn to Chapter 12, "Public Relations," in *Start-Up Basics*.

- *Brochures:* A professionally printed brochure that describes your services and background is something you might want to look into as your business becomes more successful. However, producing such a piece of collateral can be pricey and tricky. First, if you aren't a skilled writer, hiring one can cost up to a dollar a word ($17 for that last sentence, not including this comment). A professional desktop publisher will charge $200 for a black-and-white brochure, depending on the size. And having 1,000 full-color copies printed will set you back at least another $400.

The next problem is figuring out exactly what information you would put in your brochure. Most clients hire information consultants on a confidential basis, so you won't be able to list them. Even if you can publish the names of your clients, you could run into problems with companies that won't hire you because you've worked for a competitor. A full-color brochure is best left until after you have achieved a certain amount of fame in the field. When you have been quoted in magazines, written articles or books, spoken at conventions, and accumulated many years of experience, you can shoot the moon with a promotional piece. Until then, keep your costs down and your nose to the grindstone.

Does It Pay to Advertise?

If you are thinking about placing a print ad in a magazine that targets the same field as your information consulting business, take the time to do some research to make sure you're advertising in the right place. If you are hoping to have computer software companies as clients, find a magazine that addresses them specifically. But be careful here. If you want computer software companies as your clients, it won't do you much good to place an ad in a magazine for software consumers. Likewise, if your targeted clients are pharmaceutical companies, it probably won't be in your best interest to advertise in publications for pharmacists. The *Architectural Review*, for example, would be a great place to advertise if your potential clients are architects, but not the best place to advertise your services to companies that make software for architects.

If you decide that a particular magazine is an appropriate place for you to buy print advertising space, look to see whether the publication has a "marketplace" section. That's the

Smart Tip

Tip...

Prices for magazine ads are based on a term called CPM, which stands for cost per thousand. When big marketing companies place ads, they ask for the CPM, or how much it costs for each 1,000 readers to see the ad. Divide the price of the ad by the number of subscribers in thousands (15,000 becomes 15) and you have the CPM.

section in the back of the magazine where companies place one-eighth- or one-ninth-page black-and-white ads—in other words, the inexpensive section. Ad space in this section is often very reasonably priced at $100 to $400, depending on the circulation of the magazine. Add in another $250 or so to have a designer create a little text-only, black-and-white advertisement. Keep the ad simple and to the point. You'll have to test the ad to see if it works for the market you're targeting. Try it out for a month or two and see what happens. Every field is different, so don't sign a contract to run your ad for a year at a reduced monthly rate until you see some results. Even the smallest market that is profitable for a publishing company to serve (around 15,000) adds up to a lot of eyeballs that may see your ad and need your services. So keep in mind that, unless you see tremendous results from advertising, a small black-and-white ad will be just fine. For more information about advertising, see Chapter 10, "Advertising and Marketing," in *Start-Up Basics*.

The World Wide Web: Your Own Private Infomercial

Just about everyone has a Web site these days. A Web site can be a valuable marketing tool for information consultants who have enough information about their business and capabilities to fill a computer screen. Because most ISPs give you a limited amount of space for a Web site, it makes sense to use this space to advertise your business. Remember that your Web site doesn't need to be complicated. You can hire someone to put together a bare-bones, information-only site for around $500 to $1,000.

If you decide to produce a Web site for your business, keep it strictly business. The guidelines for creating brochures and ads also apply to creating a Web site: Keep it simple; tell visitors about your services; and—for goodness sake—unless you have a lot of experience building Web sites and are really good at it, leave Web development to the experts. A sloppy Web site is every bit as bad as a sloppy resume or scribbling your contact information on the back of a cocktail napkin—maybe even worse. If it's implemented correctly, your Web site will come up on the list of search-engine results for anyone looking for information in your field. So if you decide to build it yourself and do a lousy job, there's no telling how many potential clients you may alienate.

Your Web site should have information about your services and your professional experience—but not much more. It holds all the restrictions of a brochure in terms of not revealing who your clients are. But unlike a brochure, a Web site gives you the ability to provide links to full-text versions of articles you've written or quotes attributed to you on other companies' Web sites.

Bright Idea

If you are adept at learning software programs and you want to learn how to develop a Web site, buy a program that's fairly easy to use, such as Microsoft's FrontPage or Macromedia's Dreamweaver, and hack away at it in your spare time. Until you "go live" with the site (post it to a Web server), nobody will see it except you. Who knows? You may even turn Web design into a second source of income.

With most ISPs, your monthly Internet access includes a good amount of free space on which to put your Web site. The average amount of space you can use for free is around 10MB—more than enough space to tell visitors your life story and explain the services you provide. Creating a single-page site will cost you between $500 and $1,000, depending on how elaborate it is.

Another excellent way to get exposure on the Web is to join a professional organization like the AIIP. Members are listed on the association's Web site, along with brief descriptions of the services they provide.

Burwell Enterprises Inc. also publishes an annual directory of information consultants. You can order its *Burwell World Directory of Information Brokers* online (www.burwellinc.com), on a CD-ROM, or in a printed version. An abbreviated listing in the directory is free. More extensive listings, such as those featuring a link to your Web site and lengthier descriptions of the type of work you do, are available for about $75.

Seizing the Limelight

Your goal in all these marketing endeavors is to be an expert in your field of choice, someone who can not only gather information but also make sense of it. In this vein, there are two major steps you can take to show that your skills are up to par: writing magazine articles and books, and speaking at conferences. If neither of these things is in your repertoire, so be it. It's tough to get in front of people at a conference, assuming that you know more about a subject than they do, and tell them how to be better information consultants or how to better run their businesses. However, even if you don't feel up to the title of "expert," you're not completely cut out of the limelight. Most conventions have panel sessions in which people in the industry you serve discuss situations they've encountered, and the audience gets to ask questions. You don't need to have an expert opinion to be the moderator (read: referee) of a panel discussion; you just need to know enough about the subject to keep the discussion flowing.

There are also alternatives to writing full-fledged articles for publications that serve your industry. Many magazines publish annual buyer's guides that list products that are available to a particular industry. You should be subscribing to these magazines anyway, so why not offer your services to them as an information consultant? If you do a good job, you may be offered other opportunities to contribute to the magazine as a researcher or a writer. However, if you decide to write for magazines, keep in mind that some trade publications don't pay very well. You accept assignments from them based on the fact that they are giving you a byline and exposure to thousands of readers, essentially a free advertisement for your services.

> ## Smart Tip
> Tip...
>
> If you write or research a buyer's guide for a magazine, don't forget to include a way to contact you in the brief biography (usually two or three lines) that's normally included at the end of each article. It's not a good idea to put your phone number in your bio (most magazines won't even let you), but you can usually include your Web site or e-mail address.

See and Be Seen

Attending conferences is also a good way to market yourself. Whether it's a convention for information consultants or one that targets the market you serve, you'll be keeping up-to-date on the latest products, techniques, and technologies that will keep your business on the cutting edge. You'll also be surrounded by potential clients, whether they're established information consultants interested in subcontracting your services or people working in the industry you serve. The key here is to avoid a hard sell. Don't approach people who are busy working at a convention and blatantly hawk your services. Mingle. Learn about the products available. And exchange business cards with as many people as you can. When you get back to your office, make use of your other marketing materials. Add the new prospects to your mailing list and send them a press release or letter describing your services. Attending conferences is also an excellent way to find experts you can call when you need information or opinions in the course of your work.

Ultimately, the best type of marketing is to do good work in a timely and professional manner. Word gets around. As you continue to work as an information consultant, you'll find that your client base expands simply because your clients move from one company to another in the course of their careers. If you've done good work for clients in the past, who do you think they're going to call when they need to impress a new boss with a resource the chief didn't even know existed? That's right, you.

Serving Up the Information

Most information consultants work on an as-needed basis for one client at a time. But more proactive methods of finding clients, mainly by presenting information in nontraditional ways, have come into play in the past few years and are being put to use by a number of consultants. Some of the information consultants we talked to consider these presentation strategies to be marketing practices or even publishing. Whichever category you decide they fall into, these new methods of presenting information give you additional exposure and can establish you as an expert in your field. Experts get more work. So the more public you are about who you are and what you know, the more likely you are to be called upon and trusted by clients to provide accurate and timely information.

On Your Desk Every Tuesday Morning

As an information consultant, it is absolutely imperative that you know what's happening in your field of research. One way to keep abreast of developments in your industry, while at the same time establishing yourself as an expert, is to research and write an e-mail newsletter. Considered publishing by some, the e-mail newsletter allows you to gain exposure as an expert by sending your clients (and any others who want to subscribe) weekly, monthly, or bimonthly industry updates. It's best to provide information that's public but hard to keep up with—things like new product announcements, mergers, acquisitions, stock prices, and economic factors that may affect the industry. Giving out nonpublic information that you are privy to is a quick way to get sued. You should also avoid expressing opinions in your newsletter because your views could anger potential clients. Publishing factual updates on public developments in your industry will help ensure that your newsletter is objective and useful to your clients without exposing you to legal liabilities.

Here's how it works. Most companies publish their press releases on the Web. Checking the press releases from companies in your industry on a weekly basis will keep you more up-to-date than reading printed publications, so the information you gather will get to your e-mail subscribers sooner than they would normally see it. Of course, things like stock prices can be found in most major newspapers and online. But what you're trying to do is to

Bright Idea

Many marketing and public relations firms now send out press releases via e-mail to those who request them. If there are companies you want to keep track of, find out what marketing or PR firms they use and contact the firms directly to get on their press lists. Marketing or PR firms that can't e-mail the releases to you will usually send them to you via traditional mail or fax. This will help you keep track of developments in your industry.

take the effort out of your readers' information gathering. Put all the information you gather from press releases into an e-mail message you send on a regular basis. Try to send the e-mail on the same day of the week or month so readers will expect to see it.

Now you need a list of the e-mail addresses of people to send your regular industry updates to. This list may include former clients, potential clients, magazine editors who cover your field, and anyone else you think might be interested. Be sure to put the following note at the beginning of the message: "If you are not interested in receiving this industry update on a regular basis, please reply to this message with 'Unsubscribe' in the subject field." Be diligent about removing names from your list if the recipients are not interested. Remember, many people receive unwanted e-mail, or spam, all the time. You may receive a few nasty messages back from people who aren't interested. If you respond to the recipients who see your e-mail newsletter as spam, it should only be to apologize and let them know that your intentions were honorable.

An e-mail newsletter can be distributed in a number of ways. You can send it out for free as a marketing tool, or you can ask for contributions to its production, making it an informational product of its own. Ralph G., an information consultant in Abbotsford, British Columbia, started out sending his e-mail newsletter for free with a message at the end saying, "If you'd like to support the production of this newsletter, please send a donation of $15 to...." He now has approximately 11,000 readers

Bright Idea

To get a better idea of how to put together an electronic newsletter, it helps to subscribe to some. The site www.liszt.com—which has changed its name to Topica—delivers more than 100,000 e-mail newsletters or discussion groups; in the latter, a group of individuals e-mails the entire mailing list for comments.

Spam, Spam, Spam

Unsolicited e-mail, or spam, can be a problem for you even if the people you're sending it to want to receive it. To combat spam, many ISPs now have rules about how many recipients can be listed for a single e-mail message. This means that even if you have 2,000 people who want to subscribe to your weekly industry newsletter, your ISP may not let you e-mail your updates. If you have any intention of producing an e-mail newsletter—or even something as innocuous as sending out a survey to a large number of people—be sure your ISP will allow you to send it.

using four languages in 72 countries—almost all these readers gained through word-of-mouth or by readers forwarding his weekly updates to others.

Selling Your Smarts on the Web

Another way to make money from doing research is to compile extensive industry reports and sell them on the Web. Most of the companies involved in this practice are large, well-established information companies. But as the Web expands and we see more and more products and services sold directly to consumers, this approach is becoming an option for independent information consultants. If small greeting card companies are competing with Hallmark by selling their products directly, why not create an information product and sell it the same way?

First off, you'll need to have a Web page, which you may already be considering for marketing purposes. Then, of course, you'll need to create a product. As with an e-mail newsletter, start with your field of expertise and research things like current trends and market information. You might even compile an annual or biannual report on the state of the industry. Perhaps you know what information most people in your client base are looking for based on the types of projects you've been taking on. After creating an in-depth report that you think may be of value to existing and potential clients, pick out some choice morsels of information to give away as teasers and post them on your Web site, along with the report's table of contents.

From here, there are two ways to approach selling your report. If you moonlight as a Webmaster or don't mind forking over a fairly large chunk of money to create a more complex site, you can sell the report over the Internet directly. Electronic documents can be sold and downloaded online in the same manner as software products and other electronic media. Assuming this Web-based sales method is profitable for you, you could even set up a site that accepts credit cards or offers subscriptions to frequent users of your data, giving them instant access to your information. This type of Web site will become easier to set up as more small businesses decide to sell their products and services globally via the Internet.

The second, more low-tech method is to post the same teaser information on a Web site and provide contact information through which potential clients can call and buy the report from you, either as a printed document or as an e-mailed file.

In either case, featuring industry reports for sale on your Web site offers

Bright Idea

If you decide to offer information on the Web, try to find other Web sites you can share a link to and from. A link is a graphic or a line of text that someone on another Web site can click on to go directly to your site. Look for Web sites that have complementary information. Maybe you have information on sales trends for certain software and the other site has reviews of software. You get the picture.

Virtual Publicity

It's much easier now than it was 20 years ago to gain recognition as an expert. Before the Internet came into vogue, a person essentially had to get articles published in magazines to get exposure. Now, with a little time, a lot of knowledge, and a Web site, you can self-publish articles and overviews about your field of research and sell information online. But you have to be good. You have to excel not just at marketing, which is important in itself, but at finding and organizing information. The same Web site that gives you access to the millions of people on the Internet can also expose you as a hack and kill your business.

While the danger of looking like a fool to thousands of people is inherent in posting information on the Web, one of the benefits is that the information on your Web site doesn't have to stand in history forever, as it does in magazine articles and books. If you're called on a mistake or an inaccuracy, you can correct it and repost the information to the Web. But don't use this capability as an excuse to post sloppy data. Just think of it as a benefit that can help in an emergency.

numerous benefits even if you don't sell a thousand copies of each report. First, people searching the Internet for the type of information you provide could stumble upon your Web site. If they are corporate types, they might decide to call you and let you do the project for them. Or they might save your name and contact information in case they have a more complicated research project later on for which they lack the human resources or expertise. Another very real possibility is that your data may be quoted in magazines—giving you yet more exposure and a greater chance of landing more projects or selling more copies of your report.

Your success in using either sales method will depend on the quality and validity of the information you offer, as well as your own credentials. Be sure to include biographical material so potential clients will know your background, as well as a statement about the quality of the data and how it was gathered. As far as data quality goes, don't give away the whole story—just a general reference to how it was collected; include a disclaimer stating that even though the resources were checked as thoroughly as possible, you hold no liability for its use. Just to be safe, it might be a good idea to consult a lawyer to determine the exact wording to use to prevent legal problems that could result from errors.

9

Living with
the Inevitable

Taxes are a fact of life for all of us. Whether or not we feel they're fair, they need to be paid to keep the IRS from imposing untold difficulties on our lives. Because most information consultants work solo, they pretty much have to keep track of everything themselves, which can amount to a significant amount of time spent following the money. You don't get paid for keeping track of your expenses and taxes, so it makes sense to try to make the process as simple and painless as possible. That means figuring out a structure by which you can do your bookkeeping, pay your taxes, and generally keep yourself out of trouble with the IRS.

Taking Care of Business

There are many different ways to keep track of your business finances, from the ultra low-tech method of throwing receipts and pay stubs into a cigar box to be dealt with at the end of the year, to meticulously tracking every penny that comes in and goes out, using accounting software. You'll find a way to manage your finances that's comfortable for you over time. But keep in mind that once you start using a certain method, it's pretty difficult to switch to a different one. It's best to spend some time upfront, coming up with a method for tracking finances.

For some people, an old-fashioned ledger book works just fine as a means of tracking income and expenses. Make a notation in your ledger for the money that comes in and the money you spend; label and put away your receipts and pay stubs; then come up with totals each quarter and each year. Using your spreadsheet software to create a spreadsheet that has all the categories of expenses you need to track will make things a little easier. You can set up your spreadsheet to automatically add up each category or you can set up individual spreadsheets for each category. (To review the capabilities of spreadsheet programs, turn back to Chapter 5.)

The next level for tracking finances is a full-fledged accounting program, such as Intuit's QuickBooks and Peachtree Complete Accounting (designed specifically for businesses) or Microsoft's Money (a more general personal-finance package). For around $100 to $200, these programs not only keep track of your income and expenses, but also allow you to keep track of your checking, savings, and credit card accounts. If your financial institution supports online banking, you can use these programs to transfer funds, check account balances, and even pay your bills. Depending on how quickly you learn software programs, it's probably a good idea to begin using one of these applications before you start your business—maybe to keep track of your personal finances. You may even want to take a class. Once you put these programs to work, keeping everything in order is as easy as making the appropriate entries. You can also use your financial management software to print out reports for your accountant at tax time. For more information about

Bright Idea

Many accountants not only use accounting software programs but are experts in them. For a small fee, your accountant may be able to customize the categories in your accounting software for you so that all you have to do is key in the information over the course of the year. This can save you the hassle of learning everything about the program yourself.

bookkeeping and financial management, check out Chapters 14 through 16, "Book-keeping," "Financial Statements," and "Financial Management," in *Start-Up Basics*.

However you decide to keep track of your finances, remember that if you're ever audited by the IRS, you'll need to show them where, when, and how you spent your money. You shouldn't only have records, but every single receipt and pay stub. Chapter 14, "Bookkeeping," in *Start-Up Basics* has a more comprehensive list of what you should keep track of. We've provided a sample income statement on page 99 and a corresponding worksheet on page 100 to help get your record-keeping off to a good start.

Taxes Five Times a Year?

As an independent contractor, you'll have to pay your estimated taxes to Uncle Sam and any applicable state taxes four times a year, in addition to filing annual taxes. (That accountant is sounding better and better, right?) There are two ways you can figure out how much to pay in taxes, and each has its advantages and disadvantages. The first method of estimating your quarterly tax payments is to calculate actual income and expenses. The second method is to base your quarterly tax payments on the previous year's income.

Basing your tax payments on your actual income for each quarter is a good idea for a couple of reasons. First, it pretty much forces you to keep your books in order. Each quarter, you'll add up the money you earned, subtract whatever expenses you paid, and then figure out how much you owe based on the percentage for the tax bracket you're in. You'll basically have to do your taxes this way for the first year, because you really don't know how much money you're going to make. Doing your quarterlies based on actual income also makes it much easier to come up with the figures for filing your annual tax return, because all you have to do is add up the four sets of figures you came up with over the course of the year. But this method does have one danger: If you guess incorrectly about the amount of money you'll make by the end of the year and pay based on the percentage for a lower tax bracket, you can end up owing a pretty big chunk of change come the following April 15th. The obvious solution is to pick the highest tax bracket you could conceivably hit and base your quarterly payments on that amount. Sure, the government will be holding onto extra money that could be earning you interest, but it's better to be safe than sorry. If you overpay, consider the refund your annual bonus.

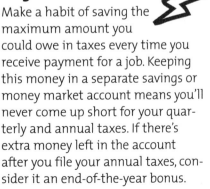

Bright Idea
Make a habit of saving the maximum amount you could owe in taxes every time you receive payment for a job. Keeping this money in a separate savings or money market account means you'll never come up short for your quarterly and annual taxes. If there's extra money left in the account after you file your annual taxes, consider it an end-of-the-year bonus.

Paying quarterly taxes based on the previous year's income also has its benefits. With this method, you merely figure out how much you paid the previous year, divide it by four, and make four equal payments. One advantage to this method is that it's easier and less time-consuming than painstakingly going over your books each quarter. After a few years, if your business is consistent or consistently increases, this method may work well for you. Just remember that if you make more money, you'll have to make up the difference by paying more on your annual return. Another disadvantage to this method is that if you end up making less in a given quarter, you still need to make the same payment no matter how painful it is. That's why this method is better after you have a few years of work under your belt and a few dollars in the bank. One great benefit of using this method comes when you make more money than you did the previous year. If you're keeping track of the situation and setting aside money for the extra payment you'll have to make on your annual taxes, there's no reason you can't invest the extra tax money or put it into an account where it will gain interest. Just make sure you can get the money out in time to pay your annual taxes.

My Life as a Deduction

There's a widely held misconception that self-employed people get to deduct just about every aspect of their lives as business expenses. Don't believe the hype. You want to spend the appropriate amount of money to keep your business in good shape, but overspending—even on deductible items—is wasting money. Yes, you do get to deduct expenses like computer equipment, office supplies, and the like because they are necessary for your job. However, if you do the math, these deductions really only amount to a discount on expenses. Say you're way up there in the 28 percent tax bracket and you decide to buy a $1,000 chair. You spend the thousand dollars on the chair and use it as a deduction. All you have saved is the 28 percent tax on that thousand dollars, which means you still spent $720 to keep your tush in the lap of luxury.

In the case of legitimate business meals, you can only claim 50 percent of the bill as an expense. Spend $200 on a meal, and the deduction has really only given you a $28 discount. The point here is not to go crazy with expenses. The fact that you get a break by not having to pay taxes on money you legitimately spend to run your business shouldn't tempt you to overspend. In the case of the chair, you're still out $720, and in the case of the meal, you're still out $172. Just a little food for thought.

Smart Tip

Tip...

If you have business-meal expenses, be sure to keep track of whom you went out with and what type of business you discussed—and save the receipt. Without this information, the IRS has no idea whether you were really at a business lunch and may disallow the deduction if you are audited.

It's also really important to make sure you don't accidentally deduct expenses that were billed to a client. Information consultants typically bill their clients for all expenses incurred in tracking down the requested information. These include fees for online services that charge hourly, long-distance phone calls, and travel expenses. It can be helpful to actually mark the bills you receive, maybe put a check mark next to things you charged the client for. The main point to keep in mind is that expenses the client has already been charged for cannot be taken as deductions.

Something else that can trip you up around tax time is your credit card. Things such as Internet access show up on your credit card every month and are legitimate business expenses. But credit card use can be confusing if you record a purchase twice—once after you make a purchase and once after you get the credit card statement. If you use the recommended "cash" (not "accrual") method of bookkeeping, you record the expense only when you pay your credit card bill and properly take just one, not two, deductions. Fortunately, credit cards can also provide a useful bit of insurance: If you

Income Statement

Doe Information Services
INCOME STATEMENT
For the Month of January 2004

Monthly Income	
Monthly collections	$7,500
Gross Monthly Profit	$7,500
*Monthly Expenses**	
ISP fee	$25
Phone	50
Postage/delivery	75
Transcription service	200
Taxes	2,100
Legal services	100
Accounting services	100
Transportation	50
Magazine subscriptions/books	30
Business meals	40
Total Monthly Expenses	**$2,770**
Net Monthly Profit	**$4,730**

*Online database access fees are not included because they are billed to the client.

lose a receipt, you still have a record of the expense on your credit card statement.

Setting up a meeting with a good accountant to discuss your taxes can be absolutely invaluable. Most information consultants hire an accountant at the end of the year to fill out their tax forms and make sure they're paying enough taxes and getting all the deductions they deserve. The point here is that it's the job of a qualified accountant to keep track of changes in tax laws and make sense of all those

Dollar Stretcher

Training, whether through school or conventions, can often be used as a tax deduction if it benefits your business. Check with your accountant to see if you can take advantage of this tax break.

forms. It's your job to be an information consultant. If you decide to file your taxes on your own, be extremely careful. One mistake can cost you a lot of money. More important, it can cost you a lot of time that you could be spending earning money.

For more information on business tax deductions and other tax-related issues, turn to Chapter 17, "Taxes," in *Start-Up Basics*.

Income Statement Worksheet

INCOME STATEMENT

For the Month of _____

Monthly Income

    Monthly collections $_____

Gross Monthly Profit $_____

Monthly Expenses

    ISP fee $_____

    Phone $_____

    Postage/delivery $_____

    Transcription service $_____

    Taxes $_____

    Legal services $_____

    Accounting services $_____

    Transportation $_____

    Magazine subscriptions/books $_____

    Business meals $_____

Total Monthly Expenses $_____

Net Monthly Profit $_____

The Secrets
to Success

s in any type of business, many factors can contribute to your success or failure. From reading this guide, you should now have a good idea of what it takes to be an information consultant. In this chapter, we take a look at the factors that can either lead you to success or cause you to look for a new day job.

The Skills and the Money

The biggest factors contributing to a new information consultant's success or failure are skills and money. Most information consultants will tell you that hardly anyone comes into the business with all the skills they need to be successful. You need to have marketing, research, bookkeeping, interviewing, and computer skills. Gaining all these skills takes time, and while you learn the ropes you are either not getting paid at all or you're making a minimal income that few can survive on. As with any business, you need to be prepared to survive on a pretty slim income for at least the first two years, even if you come into the profession with a high skill level.

What can you do to stay afloat financially during the first two years? Alternative sources of income are as varied as the services that information consultants provide. Some new information consultants have other skills they can use to supplement their incomes. These skills range from desktop publishing and journalism to engineering. Ideally, your alternative source of income should keep you close to the market you intend to serve and leave you available for clients during business hours. Some information consultants rely on the financial support of spouses while their businesses get started. Others borrow money from their family or friends. Still others save up the money they'll need or leave their jobs and cash in their retirement plans (a pretty dangerous move, by the way). Wherever this extra money comes from, you need it. You can't expect to come out of the chute making the same amount of money you did working at a full-time job in Corporate America.

There are those who think it's fine to avoid putting away money for their golden years for a while as they get their businesses up and running. If you choose this path, remember that you also lose the accompanying tax benefits and interest. Unless you really have no other way to buy your freedom, keeping your retirement fund intact is a good idea. These funds are usually not subject to income tax unless you liquidate them, and the rate at which they grow can be a pleasant surprise amidst your struggles to start a new business.

"I had about $12,000 in a retirement fund," Amelia K., the information consultant in Sebastopol, California, told us. "I decided not to cash it in and got a $15,000 loan instead. I'm really glad I didn't cash it in because all those years I was struggling, I couldn't really put any money away. In the 20 years since I started, that money has really grown. For me, it was better to get a loan even though it was scarier. I always knew I had that money to fall back on."

The overall cost to get started as an information consultant may not look very high at first glance. However, you also need

Bright Idea

There's no rule that says you have to make your entire living as an information consultant. Keep editing, desktop publishing, Web design, and whatever else you know how to do in your bag of tricks. Make sure others know of these skills and offer them for a fee. You may even find that a large number of information consultants are your clients in these other endeavors.

to factor in the time and money for taking classes if you need to gain computer skills or online research skills. Whether or not you have paying work, there will be plenty to keep your checkbook busy—things like taking classes, practicing your craft, and trying to make a name for yourself. There are even seminars that will teach you the basics of being an information consultant, but they aren't cheap.

Another big financial question involves benefits. You need to have health insurance. Individual health insurance plans can be very expensive, but not having one can be even more expensive. Health care may be the single biggest reason many people are reluctant to go into business for themselves. Even with the COBRA law, which allows you to keep the insurance you have when you leave your job, you'll be paying not only the monthly premium that used to come out of your paycheck but also the share your employer paid. In many cases, this can more than triple the cost of staying insured. Having a spouse or family member who can cover you on his or her policy can be a big help. (For more on insurance, turn to Chapter 6, "Employees, Benefits, and Policies," in *Start-Up Basics*.)

Building a Solid Foundation

To succeed as an information consultant, you need to be a specialist. Even if you're planning to subcontract work from established information consultants, you need a specific area of expertise. (It should be noted that those consultants you hope to subcontract from will probably be even harder to impress than corporate clients.) It's true that many information consultants serve more than one audience, but that's something you should think about after you've been in the business for a while. Get to know all the players by joining a professional organization and subscribing to every magazine, newsletter, or other publication that has information about the field you intend to serve. Find out who is providing this industry with information services and try to talk to those companies or individuals about the ins and outs of the industry—even if you have to pay for the information.

Most of all, be honest with yourself about what you're good at and what you enjoy doing. If you don't feel comfortable with a certain aspect of information consulting, find others who are not only good at it but enjoy it, and subcontract work to them. If you're honest with yourself, you have a much better chance of making it in this or any other business. If your problem is a lack of knowledge or training, seek out the information you need and pay for the training.

The Company You'll Keep

If you survive your first few years and realize that you are happy and making money, congratulations! You're a card-carrying member of an elite group of entrepreneurs in one of the newest and fastest-growing professions. Be sure that you enjoy the work. The thrill of digging up information can be gratifying and very challenging at the same time. The work will get easier as you gain more skills, but it will never be easy. If it were, everyone

> ## ⚠ Beware!
>
> If you don't have an alternate means of financial support such as friends or family to fall back on, you'll have to rely on savings to get started as an information consultant. Be realistic about when to throw in the towel. No one says you can't build up your savings and give it another go sometime in the future.

who needed information would just dig it up themselves, and you would be reading a guide about how to start a different kind of business.

Information consultants are generally a very friendly and helpful bunch. They communicate with each other, ask each other for help, and subcontract work to others, not because the work is beneath them, but because someone else is better at doing the job. Keep this in mind as you enter the profession. Information consultants are quite proud of the skills they've acquired and very protective of the world's perception of the services they provide. You can get a bad name in the industry quickly by doing sloppy work or by charging too little for your services. Word travels fast because it's difficult for the next consultant to sell his or her services to a company after that company has been burned or has gotten too good a deal because you were desperate for the work. Making these types of mistakes will hurt you in the future—not only by souring your relationships with clients and your professional peers, but also by clouding the world's perception of information consulting.

Shut Down or Search On?

The biggest danger in starting a business as an information consultant is running out of money before you have a chance to find out whether you can be successful. Assume that you will make little or no money the first year and keep an eye on whether things are looking up significantly during your second year. Only you can decide how long you want to keep at it before you give up and move on to some other—maybe even related—profession. If you are not responsible for the mortgage payments or rent, health benefits, and so on, you'll still need to justify the time you spend building your information consulting business with the person who is providing the financial support.

There are a number of warning signs that you may need to find a different profession. If, after two years, you still find that you are working a lot of nights and weekends and don't have the time or money for vacations, you are going to be an unhappy person. Unhappy people usually do lousy work, however much they fool themselves into putting on a happy face for their clients. If you reach this point and you have made every effort to learn the skills you need, try taking a time-management class. If your life is still a roller coaster of late nights and missed parties, consider other options. Remember that even if you leave the information consulting profession, you'll probably come out of it with important skills that will be valuable to employers. A failed business venture is still a business venture, and the lessons and skills you'll have learned will be impressive. Good luck!

Appendix
Information Consultant Resources

They say you can never be too rich or too thin. While these could be argued, we believe you can never have enough resources. Therefore, we present for your consideration a wealth of sources for you to check into, check out, and harness for your own personal information blitz.

These sources are tidbits, ideas to get you started on your research. They are by no means the only sources out there, and they should not be taken as the ultimate answer. We have done our research, but businesses do tend to move, change, fold, and expand. As we have repeatedly stressed, do your homework. Get out, and start investigating.

Associations

The American Association of Law Libraries, 53 W. Jackson, #940, Chicago, IL 60604, (312) 939-4764, www.aallnet.org

American Library Association, 50 E. Huron, Chicago, IL 60611, (800) 545-2433, www.ala.org

American Medical Informatics Association, 4915 St. Elmo Ave., #401, Bethesda, MD 20814, (301) 657-1291, www.amia.org

American Society for Information Science, 1320 Fenwick Ln., #510, Silver Spring, MD 20910, (301) 495-0900, www.asis.org

▲

The Association of Independent Information Professionals, 8550 United Plaza Blvd., #1001, Baton Rouge, LA 70809, (225) 408-4400, www.aiip.org

Association of Information and Dissemination Centers, P.O. Box 3212, Maple Glen, PA 19002-8212, (215) 654-9129, www.asidic.org

The Electronic Frontier Foundation, 454 Shotwell St., San Francisco, CA 94110, (415) 436-9333, www.eff.org

Medical Library Association, 65 E. Wacker Pl., #1900, Chicago, IL 60601-7298, (312) 419-9094, www.mlahq.org

The National Federation of Abstracting and Information Services, 1518 Walnut St., #307, Philadelphia, PA 19102-3403, (215) 893-1561, www.nfais.org

Research Libraries Group, 1200 Villa St., Mountain View, CA 94041-1100, (650) 691-2333, www.rlg.org

Society of Competitive Intelligence Professionals, 1700 Diagonal Rd., #600, Alexandria, VA 22314, (703) 739-0696, www.scip.org

Special Libraries Association, 1700 18th St. NW, Washington, DC 20009-2514, (202) 234-4700, www.sla.org

Books

The Burwell World Directory of Information Brokers, Burwell Enterprises, 30 Fairway Park, Montgomery, TX 77356, (936) 597-3224, www.burwellinc.com

County Court Records, BRB Publications, P.O. Box 27869, Tempe, AZ 85285, (800) 929-3811, www.brbpub.com

Find It Online, Alan M. Schein, Facts on Demand Press, P.O. Box 27869, Tempe, AZ 85285, (800) 929-3811, www.brbpub.com

How to Avoid Liability: The Information Professional's Guide to Negligence and Warrant Risks, T.R. Halvorson, Burwell Enterprises, 30 Fairway Park, Montgomery, TX 77356, (936) 597-3224, www.burwellinc.com

Legal Liability Problems in Cyberspace: Craters in the Information Highway, T.R. Halvorson, Burwell Enterprises, 30 Fairway Park, Montgomery, TX 77356, (936) 597-3224, www.burwellinc.com

Naked in Cyberspace: How to Find Personal Information Online, Carole A. Lane, Information Today, 143 Old Marlton Pike, Medford, NJ 08055-8750, (800) 300-9868, www.infotoday.com

Online Competitive Intelligence, Helen Burwell, Facts on Demand Press, P.O. Box 27869, Tempe, AZ 85285, (800) 929-3811, www.brbpub.com

Public Records Online, Michael Sankey and Peter Weber, Facts on Demand Press, P.O. Box 27869, Tempe, AZ 85285, (800) 929-3811, www.brbpub.com

Sawyer's Success Tactics for Information Businesses, Deborah C. Sawyer, Burwell Enterprises, 30 Fairway Park, Montgomery, TX 77356, (936) 597-3224, www.burwellinc.com

Sawyer's Survival Guide for Information Brokers, Deborah C. Sawyer, Burwell Enterprises, 30 Fairway Park, Montgomery, TX 77356, (936) 597-3224, www.burwellinc.com

The MVR Book 2003, BRB Publications, P.O. Box 27869, Tempe, AZ 85285, (800) 929-3811, www.brbpub.com

Magazines and Other Periodicals

EContent and *ONLINE*, Online Inc., 213 Danbury Rd., Wilton, CT 06897-4007, (800) 248-8466, www.econtentmag.com

The Guide to Background Investigations and Public Record Searching, (book/CD), BRB Publications, P.O. Box 27869, Tempe, AZ 85285, (800) 929-3811, www.brbpub.com

Information Today, 143 Old Marlton Pike, Medford, NJ 08055-8750, (800) 300-9868, www.infotoday.com

Searcher, Information Today Inc.,143 Old Marlton Pike, Medford, NJ 08055-8750, (800) 300-9868, www.infotoday.com

Mentor Programs and Seminars

The Association of Independent Information Professionals, 8550 United Plaza Blvd., #1001, Baton Rouge, LA 70809, (225) 408-4400, www.aiip.org Online Databases

Burwell Enterprises, 30 Fairway Park, Montgomery, TX 77356, (936) 597-3224, www.burwellinc.com

MarketingBase Mentor, 1364 Kathy Ln., Sebastopol, CA 95472, (800) 544-5924, (707) 829-9421, www.marketingbase.com

Online Databases

Burrelle's Information Services, 75 E. Northfield Rd., Livingston, NJ 07039, (800) 631-1160, (973) 992-6600, www.burrelles.com

The Dialog Corp., 11000 Regency Pkwy., #10,Cary, NC 27511, (800) 3-DIALOG or (919) 462-8600, www.dialog.com

Investext, 3818 Westwick Trace, Kennesaw, GA 30152, (770) 428-9727, www.investext.com

LexisNexis, P.O. Box 933, Dayton, OH 45401-0933, (800) 227-4908, www.lexisnexis.com

▲

ProQuest Information and Learning, 300 N. Zeeb Rd., Ann Arbor, MI 48106, (800) 521-0600, www.umi.com

Questel-Orbit, 8000 Westpark Dr., McLean, VA 22102, (703) 442-0900, www.questel.orbit.com

Online Listings of Information Consultants

Association of Independent Information Professionals, www.aiip.org

Burwell Enterprises, www.burwellinc.com

Successful Information Consulting Firms

Ardito Information & Research Inc., Stephanie Ardito, 1019 Sedwick Dr., Ste. G, Wilmington, DE 19803, (800) 836-9068, (302) 479-5373, www.ardito.com

Information Matters, Pamela Wegmann, 17 Chalstrom Dr., New Orleans, LA 70123, www.info-matters.com

Inquix Consulting Limited, J. Derek Pugsley, 17069 Innis Lake Rd., RR #1, Caledon East, Ontario, CAN L0N 1E0, (800) 461-5807, (905) 584-2196, www.inquix.com

MarketingBase Mentor, Amelia Kassel, 1364 Kathy Lane, Sebastopol, CA 95472, (800) 544-5924, (707) 829-9421, www.marketingbase.com

TechnoSearch Inc., Carole Lane, P.O. Box 3729, Vista, CA 92085-3739, (760) 806-4800, www.technosearch.com

upFront.eZine Publishing Ltd., Ralph Grabowski, 34486 Donlyn Ave., Abbotsford, BC, V2S 4W7, (604) 859-9597, www.upfrontezine.com

Glossary

Boolean operators: words or symbols placed between keywords to identify relationships between them and help search engines return more accurate results; common Boolean operators are AND, NEAR, and OR.

Cable modem: a device that allows users to send data over cable lines at speeds of up to 3.8 mbps.

CD-R drive: Compact Disc Recordable drive; a disc drive that allows users not only to read data stored on CD-ROM discs, but also to record data onto blank compact discs called CD-R discs.

CD-ROM drive: Compact Disc Read Only Memory drive; a disk drive that allows users to read files and software applications from a CD-ROM disc and copy these onto a computer's hard drive.

CD-RW drive: Compact Disk Rewritable drive; a disc drive that lets users not only read data stored on CD-ROM discs but also copy data to a special type of compact disc called a CD-RW disc, which can be erased and recorded over multiple times.

Compatibility: the ability for files created on one computer to be viewed and changed on another computer that is running the same software.

▲

Contact manager: a software program that stores information about people—such as names, addresses, and phone numbers—in a specially formatted database.

Database: an organized, logically structured "warehouse" of computer-accessible information, such as customer data Digital Subscriber Line: *see* DSL.

DSL: Digital Subscriber Line; technology for sending data over the copper wires in telephone lines at speeds of up to 7.1MB/ second.

E-mail newsletter: an electronic newsletter sent at a scheduled time to interested readers.

Flat rate: work done based on a fee agreed upon before a job is started, rather than by the hour.

Integrated Services Digital Network: *see* ISDN.

Internet Service Provider: see *ISP.*

ISDN: Integrated Services Digital Network; technology for sending data over specially installed digital telephone lines at speeds of up to 144KB/second.

ISP: Internet Service Provider; a company that sells access to a computer called an Internet server, which provides access to e-mail and the Internet.

Multifunction device: a device that can scan, copy, print, and fax.

Online service: a dial-in or Internet database or subscription service such as Dialog or LexisNexis, in which the user pays for the time spent accessing information; this term is also used by some ISPs to indicate that they offer more benefits than basic Web and e-mail access.

Primary research: the process of contacting people directly for information; *see* secondary research.

Quarterly tax payment: self-employed people in the United States are required to make estimated tax payments on specified dates four times a year in addition to annual tax returns.

Repetitive-stress injuries: painful musculoskeletal maladies caused by doing the same thing over and over again, such as typing or using a mouse.

Secondary research: the process of gathering information from published sources; *see* primary research.

Spam: unwanted e-mail sent to large numbers of uninterested recipients.

Tape drive: a device that copies data to high-capacity magnetic tape cartridges for backup purposes.

Web browser: a software program that allows users to view the graphical information on the World Wide Web.

Word processing software: an application that allows users to type in data and format it in various ways.

Zip drive: a disk drive created by Iomega that uses special high-capacity disks that hold up to 750MB of data.

Index

A

Accountant, hiring an, 21, 27, 96, 100

Accounting
   ledger, 96–97
   software, 96–97

Advertising, 81–93
   magazine and print, 86–87
   paid, 86–87

Appendix, 105–108

Articles, writing professional, 25, 88–89

B

Backgrounds of those entering the information consulting profession, 2, 5–7

Benefits, paying for self and employee, 103

Bidding for jobs, 18
   flat *vs.* hourly rate, 65

Billing, 23, 66

Bookkeeper, hiring a, 21

Bookkeeping, 96–97

Books, list of recommended, 106–107

Boolean searches, 74–77

Brochure
   printing of, 83
   professional, 83, 86
   your Web site as online, 87–88

Business background, 6

Business card, 82–83

Business start-up, financial demands of, 5

Buyer's guides, compiling magazine, 8, 89

C

Caller ID, 44

CD-R drive, 36, 40

CD-ROM drives, 36, 40

Cell phones, 44–45

Cheat sheet, 72–73

Client
   contact software, 53–54
   contracts, 13–14, 22, 63
   deadbeat, 64
   ex-employer as first, 5, 81
   face-to-face meetings with, 29–30, 31
   formatting information for, 25, 80

manager software programs, 53–54
meetings, 9, 24, 71
presenting a professional appearance
    when meeting, 71
referrals, 6–7
Colleagues, networking with your, 16–17,
    103–104
Competition
    joining forces with your, 16–17
    researching your, 16–18
Complementary skills, teaming up with a
    group and providing, 27
Computer
    backup devices and firewalls, 38–41
    choosing a, 34
    considerations, 34–37
    literacy, 4, 9
    monitor, 35
    printer, 41–42
    products, list of online stores, 39
    security issues, 37
    software, 47–55
Conferences, speaking at, 25, 107
Confidentiality, 12, 18, 22
Contact manager software programs, 53–54
Contracts, written, 13–14, 22, 63
Copier, 43
Corporate research on competitors, 8, 12–13

D

Database
    development services, 80
    online, 17, 24, 79, 107–108
    pay-as-you-go, 76, 79
    software programs, 53
    sophistication of, 70
    specialized, 79
Day in the life of an information consult-
    ant, 20–25
Deadlines, meeting, 9
Deductions, tax, 98–100
Delegating, 21
Domain name, 32

E

E-mail
    and phone contact, using in tandem, 78

correspondence, 20–21
    fax service via, 44
    programs, 50–51
    unsolicited, 91
E-search shortcuts, 73
Electronic
    devices, 33–46
    newsletter as marketing tool, 90–92
Emergency rush jobs, 24
Employees
    benefits, 103
    family members as, 26
    hiring, 27–28
    working from their own home offices, 28
Ex-employer as first client, 5, 81
Expanding your business, 27
Expenses, monthly, 61–62
Expertise
    exploring markets for your, 16
    finding your area of, 5–7
    previous, 6–7
    selling your, 88–89, 90, 93
Experts, interviewing, 22

F

Fax
    machine, 42
    service via email, 44
Final report, presentation of, 80
Financial
    backup, starting out with, 102–103, 104
    information, researching corporate, 73
    recordkeeping, 96–100
    research into potential corporate buy-
        outs/mergers, 13
Firewalls, hardware vs. software, 42
Flat rate vs. hourly rate, 65
Focusing your search, 70–71
Frequent flier miles, 61, 62

G

Gadgets and gizmos, 33–46
Glossary, 109–111
Government listings, online, 73

H

Hard drive, 35

Homebased business, 9, 28–32
    compliance with zoning regulations,
        30–31
    tax advantages of, 30
    workspace, 31–32
Hourly rates, determining your, 63–65

I

Inhouse research staffs, 18
Income potential, 9, 62–67
    annually, 67–68
Income statement
    sample of, 99
    worksheet, 100
Industry
    overviews, producing and selling, 27
    reports, compiling and selling on the
        Web, 92
Industry organizations
    finding clients through, 82
    researching, 73
Information
    explosion, 17
    filtering, 7
    formatting into a readable report for
        client, 25
    inaccurate, 77
Information consulting firms, list of, 108
Internet
    and ease of access to online informa-
        tion, 2
    billions of pages of information on, 10
    connections, types of, 37–38
    research, 70–79
    resources, less obvious, 78
    savvy, 4, 9
    server, backing up data to "hot sites,"
        38
    service provider (ISP) choosing a,
        48–50
    service provider (ISP) monthly expense
        of, 48–50
    Web browsers, 50 (See also Online,
        Web)
Invoice, 23
    sample of, 66

L

Laptop computers, 36–37
Lawyer, hiring a, 13–14, 22, 63, 93
Legal research, 5, 8
Liability, hiring lawyers to cover oneself
    against potential, 13–14, 22, 63, 93
Library
    background as head start, 15
    research skills, 3, 9
    research trips, 24
Location, 28–32
    cost of living and quality of life consid-
        erations, 29

M

Magazines
    industry and trade, 22, 73
    list of, 107
Marketing, 24, 90–92. See also Advertising
Markets
    finding your niche, 15
    for your services, 11–18
    researching potential, 14–16
Medical patients, researching conditions
    and treatments for, 13–14
Medical researcher
    background of, 6
    for medical supply and pharmaceutical
        companies, 13, 15
Mentor programs, 2, 6, 107
Money, running out of, 104
Monitor, computer, 35

N

Naming your business, 32
Networking, 23
Newsletter
    as marketing tool, 90–92
    subscriptions, 22
Newspaper archives, searching online, 73
Niche
    importance of finding your, 103
    markets, targeting, 15

O

Office equipment, 33–46
    buying with a credit card, 61

checklist, sample of, 46
expenses, list of, 60
start-up expenses, 58–61
upgrading *vs.* buying new, 58–59
Office space, renting, 59
Office supplies, bulk buying of, 25
Online databases, 17, 24
sophistication of, 70
specialized, 79 (*See also* Database, Internet, Web)
Organized, ability to be, 4

P

Pagers, 44–45
Paper costs, 61
Paperwork, taking care of, 22
Part-time profession, 5
Partnerships, 26
Patent information, researching, 8, 10
People skills, 3
Personal background information
researching, 14
Web sites geared toward, 14
Pharmaceutical industry, largesse of, 15
Phone number Web searches, 14
Prerequisites before you start, 9
Presentation methods, 25, 80
Press release, 84–86, 90–91
sample of, 85
Printer, computer, 41–42
Product information research, 13
Professional associations
listing of, 105–106
membership, 6, 16
Project overlap, 79
Promoting your business, 81–93
Promotional pieces, 83–86
Public speaking, 88–89
Publicity, virtual, 93
Publishing company research for untapped
magazine or newsletter markets, 8–9

Q

Questions to ask to determine if you are
suited to the profession, 3

R

RAM, 35

Reading as integral part of the job, 3
Recordkeeping, 95–98
Reference materials, wealth of, on and
offline, 10. *See also* Research
Referral
of colleagues, 30 (*See also* Subcontracting)
programs, professional association's, 6
Rejection, accepting, 4
Repetitive stress injuries, preventing,
59–60
Report, creating a "client friendly," 25, 80
Research
aptitude for, 3
corporate, 8, 12–13, 73
inhouse, 18
internet, 70–79
legal, 5, 8
library, 24
primary, 21–22, 76
telephone, 24, 26
tools, availing oneself of all available, 76
Resources
for information consultants, 105–108
pooling with other information consultants, 27
Rush jobs, 24

S

Sales letters, 83–84
sample of, 84
Scanner, 43
Search engine
Boolean searches on, 74–77
capabilities, 73–77
Self-confidence, 4
Self-discipline, 4
Seminars, 2, 107
Skills
as crucial factor in success, 102
of Information consultants, 3–5
Small claims court, taking clients to, 64
Snail mail promotion, 83–86
Software
checklist, sample of, 55
financial management, 54
office suite packages, 54
options, 47–55

paying for it *vs.* "borrowing" it, 51
presentation programs, 55
spreadsheet, 52–53
Sole proprietorship, 25–26
Spam, 91
Specializations, diversity of, 5–7
Specialty, importance of developing a, 103
Spreadsheet software programs, 52–53
Stand-alone e-mail programs, 50–51. *See also* E-mail
Standards organizations, researching member companies' sites, 73
Start-up
    costs, worksheet, 9 (*See also* Office equipment expenses)
    funding, 9
Structuring your business, 25–26
Subcontracting, 16–17, 23, 26–27
    agreement, 27
    work from experienced consultants, 62
Success secrets, 101–104

T

Taxes, 96–100
    filing quarterly, 24
    to file for subcontractors, 27
Telephone
    calls, promptly returning, 21
    expenses, monthly, 61
    research, 24, 26
    research devotees, 76
    service, 43–45
    tag, avoiding, 78
Traits of information consultants, 3–5
Trends, following industry, 14
Typical business day of an information consultant, 20–25
Typing skills, 5

U

Useless leads, avoiding, 75

W

Warranties, equipment, 45
Web browsers, 50
Web site
    addresses, 76
    articles and newsletters, self-published, 93
    as marketing tool, 87, 92
    as online brochure, 87–88
    creating a business, 32
    devoted to Information Professionals, 6
    linking, 6, 92–93
Webmaster, verifying information with, 77
    (*See also* Internet, Online)
Weekly e-mail bulletins, industry specific subscriptions to, 7
When to call it quits, 104
Wireless networking, 37
Word processing programs, 51–52
Workflow, managing your, 23
Workspace, 31–32
Workstation, setting up your, 61
Worth, determining your "financial," 63–65
Writing magazine articles and books as free advertising tool, 25, 88–89
    self-published on Web site, 93
Written agreement, drafting a legally sound, 13–14, 22, 63

Z

Zoning regulations, 30–31